INTERTEXTUALITY
IN LITERATURE AND FILM

Intertextuality in Literature and Film

Selected Papers from the Thirteenth Annual
Florida State University
Conference on Literature and Film

Edited by
Elaine D. Cancalon and Antoine Spacagna

UNIVERSITY PRESS OF FLORIDA
GAINESVILLE

Library of Congress Cataloging-in-Publication Data

Florida State University Conference on Literature and Film (13th : 1988)
    Intertextuality in literature and film : selected papers from the Thirteenth
    Annual Florida State University Conference on Literature and Film / edited by
    Elaine D. Cancalon and Antoine Spacagna.
        p.   cm.
    Includes bibliographical references and index.
    ISBN 0-8130-1287-2
    1. Intertextuality—Congresses.   2. Literature, Modern—History and
    criticism—Congresses.   3. Motion pictures—Congresses.
    I. Cancalon, Elaine D. (Elaine Davis)   II. Spacagna, Antoine.
    III. Florida State University.   IV. Title.
    PN98.I58F57   1988
    809—dc20   93-38340
                                                                          CIP

Portions of John Burt Foster, Jr.'s chapter, "Starting with Dostoevsky's *Double*: Bakhtin and Nabokov
as Intertextualists," were originally published in John Burt Foster, Jr., *Nabokov's Art of Memory and
European Modernism.* Copyright 1993 by Princeton University Press. Reprinted by permission of
Princeton University Press.

The illustrations from *Benches,* by Tom Phillips, are reprinted by permission of the editor of *Works,
Texts* (Stuttgart, 1975) in Erdmute Wenzel White's chapter, "Emblematic Indirections: *Benches* by
Tom Phillips."

The University Press of Florida is the scholarly publishing agency for the State
University System of Florida, comprised of Florida A & M University, Florida
Atlantic University, Florida International University, Florida State University,
University of Central Florida, University of Florida, University of North Florida,
University of South Florida, and University of West Florida.

University Press of Florida
15 Northwest 15th Street
Gainesville, FL 32611

This volume is dedicated to Professor Emeritus Nokola Pribic of the Department of Modern Languages and Linguistics, Florida State University, who in 1968 founded the Comparative Literature Circle, which subsequently gave birth to this series of annual conferences and its resulting volumes.

ACKNOWLEDGMENTS

The essays collected here are a selection of some of the most significant papers among the nearly 270 read at the Thirteenth Annual Conference on Literature and Film sponsored by the Comparative Literature Circle of Florida State University, on the conference topic ''Intertextuality.''

We express our gratitude to the late Augustus B. Turnbull, Provost of Florida State University, for his sustained support of our conferences, and to Werner A. Baum, Dean Emeritus of the College of Arts and Sciences, for helping to make this volume possible. We wish to thank the members of the Advisory Board and the Editorial Committee. We are also grateful to the following departments, programs, and organizations which provided funds and assistance: Departments of Modern Languages and Linguistics, English, and Classics, College of Communications, Black Studies Program, Quebec Delegation in Atlanta, Women's Studies Program, and the School of Theater.

Special thanks goes to John Brennan of Florida State Center for Professional Development for his help in the organization of the conference and to Lori Howard and Andrew Kouroupis, and Roxanne Fletcher of the Philosophy Department, for their editorial assistance.

CONTENTS

1 INTRODUCTION
Elaine D. Cancalon and Antione Spacagna, *Florida State University* *1*

2 STARTING WITH DOSTOEVSKY'S DOUBLE:
BAKHTIN AND NABOKOV AS INTERTEXTUALIST
John Burt Foster, Jr., *George Mason University* *9*

3 A CHARACTER'S INDICTMENT OF AUTHORIAL
SUBTERFUGE: THE PARODY OF TEXTS IN
ROBERTO G. FERNANDEZ'S FICTION
Jorge Febles, *Western Michigan University* *21*

4 FEDERATED FANCIES:
BALZAC'S *LOST ILLUSIONS* AND MELVILLE'S *PIERRE*
Benjamin Sherwood Lawson, *Albany State College* *37*

5 TEXTS ENGENDERING TEXTS:
A QUÉBECOIS REWRITING OF AMERICAN NOVELS
Anne Marie Miraglia, *University of Toronto* *49*

6 SILONE'S "MOSES" AT THE BITTER FOUNTAIN:
EXODUS AS SUBTEXT
Marisa Gatti-Taylor, *Marquette University* *61*

7 POETRY AND LANGUAGE: INTERTEXTUALITY IN
THE WORKS OF JOSÉ ANGEL VALENTE
Anita M. Hart, *University of North Carolina, Charlotte* *75*

8 PLACING SOURCE IN *GREED* AND *MCTEAGUE*
Mary Lawlor, *Muhlenberg College 93*

9 DESICA'S *BICYCLE THIEVES* AND THE ATTACK
ON THE CLASSICAL HOLLYWOOD FILM
Gerard Molyneaux, *La Salle University 105*

10 PICTURES OF PICTURES: REFERENCE AND REALITY
IN TWO SCRIPT VERSIONS OF *POTEMKIN*
Bruce E. Fleming, *U. S. Naval Academy 127*

11 THE COMPOUND GENRE FILM: *BILLY THE KID VERSUS
DRACULA* MEETS *THE HARVEY GIRLS*
Adam Knee, *The New School for Social Research 141*

12 EMBLEMATIC INDIRECTIONS:
BENCHES, BY TOM PHILLIPS
Erdmute Wenzel White, *Purdue University 157*

INDEX *173*

1. INTRODUCTION

Elaine D. Cancalon &
Antoine Spacagna

HISTORICALLY AUTHORS HAVE ALWAYS been aware of relationships between the work they were writing and other texts. This awareness was traditionally expressed through such techniques as allusion, quotation, pastiches, parodic fragments, etc. However, for these authors the text was usually considered as a unit in itself. As Roland Barthes explains in "Theory of the Text ": "The classical sign is a sealed unit, whose closure arrests meaning, prevents it from trembling or becoming double, or wandering. The same goes for the classical text: it closes the work, chains it to its letter, rivets it to its signified."[1] Since for Barthes any text cannot be disassociated from the active work of reading, the closure he means to point out must apply to traditional exegesis (historical, biographical) for the very concept of intertextuality means that no text is an untouched, unified whole. In fact he goes on in *S/Z* to show how a polyphonic reading can be superimposed on a nineteenth-century"realist" novella. The text is a galaxy of signifiers, a network of interrelated codes, an open, dynamic playground where the endless process of signification takes place.

However, according to Mikhaïl Bakhtin, the novel has always been a "dialogic" form, combining within itself various generic expressions.

He states that "[The languages of heteroglossia] are all able to enter into the unitary plane of the novel, which can unite in itself parodic stylizations of generic languages, various forms of stylizations and illustrations of professional and period-bound languages, the languages of particular generations, of social dialects and others."[2] One can already see here how social texts imbed themselves into artistic ones and vice-versa. Although Bakhtin was already writing in the 1920s, it was not until the mid-sixties that the term "intertextuality" was coined by Julia Kristeva in her re-reading of Bakhtin: ". . . any text is constructed as a mosaic of quotations; any text is the absorption and transformation of another. In place of the notion of intersubjectivity that of intertextuality affirms itself and poetic language is read, at the very least, as a double."[3]

Kristeva's work uses Bakhtinian theories on the polyphonic novel. In this same vein, Michel Foucault proposes a definition of the "livre" (book): ". . . no book can exist by itself; it is always in a relationship of support and dependence in regard to others; it is a spot in a network; it contains a system of landmarks which refer . . . explicitly or not . . . to other books, other texts, or other sentences" (our translation).[4] As we can see, Foucault also speaks of "other texts" and Kristeva's use of the word "intertextuality" necessarily raises the question: What is a text? The concept of text is not limited to the written word. According to Barthes, a text is a semiological system: "All signifying practices can engender text: the practice of painting pictures, musical practice, filmic practice, etc. The works, in certain cases, themselves prepare the subversion of the genres, of the homogeneous classes to which they have been assigned. . . ."[5]

For all these authors, literary and artistic productions must be situated within a social context which itself can be considered as a text because social structures are the products of reading and re-readings. Societies and history have no meaning outside of the way in which they are interpreted.

As editors, our "readings and re-readings" of the selected articles led us to decide upon a certain order. This order proceeds from the written to the visual. The first four articles (Foster, Febles, Lawson, Miraglia) concentrate on intertextual analyses between novels. Gatti-Taylor's study deals with biblical realities in an Italian novel. Hart, while mentioning transposed biblical texts in the poetry of José Angel Valente, emphasizes the reflexive aspect of Valente's poems on poetry. Self-consciousness is also central to Lawlor's article which compares a novel to its cinematic adaptation. The following study (Molyneaux's) also deals with the transposition of a novel to the screen.

The position of Fleming's article is meant to show that film scripts are a *written* version of a *visual* medium. They are therefore inherently intertextual. Adam Knee studies intergeneric dynamics within the medium of cinema. The last article by E. W. White discusses modifications of an image within the realm of plastic arts.

Any volume, in order to be understandable, has to be organized according to some "structure." However, the articles themselves put into question the supposedly "logical" order of our presentation because, being intertextual, they combine discussions which subvert the very distinction between the written and the visual. After all, the studies of film are all written texts which attempt to describe, without our seeing it, a visual medium. The last article includes the visual (through reproduction) in a written volume. Poor substitute for a trip to the Tate Gallery!

A true definition of generic structures cannot incorporate specific distinctions such as the written and the visual. The reader of fiction necessarily conjures up visual images. A film contains written dialogues or narration as well as significant music, in constant interaction with the images in the spectator's ("reader's") mind. Similarly when one looks at a painting one tries to explain it through words. Works of art, like fashion, are always commented. The most minimal comment is produced by the title itself and even "Untitled" is another form of title. The reputation of the gallery is also a part of the paratext.

John Burt Foster's article "Starting with Dostoevsky's *Double*: Bakhtin and Nabokov as Intertextualists" was chosen to begin this volume because its application of Bakhtin places it at the origins of intertextual theorizing. According to Foster, both Bakhtin and Nabokov interpret Dostoevsky's *The Double* as the author's first dialogic novel, but Nabokov's parody of *The Double* in his book *Despair* focused exclusively on interaction with other texts, while Bakhtin's dialogism includes both exterior and interior discourse systems. In any case the intertextual chain is well illustrated by this voyage which takes us from Nabokov to Gogol by way of Dostoevsky. However, side excursions readily occur (e.g., Bakhtin). As Foster points out, "intertextuality involves cultural dispersion as well as transmission."

Bakhtinian theory is also the basis of Jorge Febles's study of Roberto Fernandez's fiction. He demonstrates that Fernandez's texts are polyphonic constructs and describes the parodic interactions of a recurring character, Eloy de los Reyes, and for example, Unamuno's Augusto Perez. In both cases the characters ask their narrators to further develop the story. This metalepsis illustrates the relationship between self-conscious fiction and intertextuality.

Parody of a specific text is one form of intertextuality. Nabokov and Bakhtin had both read Dostoevsky. But as Benjamin Lawson explains, the relationship between *Lost Illusions* and Melville's *Pierre* is based not on a specific rewriting, but on a common western *Zeitgeist,* of which self-consciousness is a dominant element. Narcissism is present not only in the realm of psychology, but also in artistic trends. Both of these novels are books about books and as readers we are watching ourselves consuming literary texts.

Anne Marie Miraglia's text,"Text Engendering Texts" also deals with autorepresentation in Jacques Poulin's *Volkswagen Blues*, a Quebecois rewriting of American travel novels. It illustrates the "américanité" of the Quebecois society. This rewriting, by concentrating on a minority's quest for identify, confronts that minority's discourse with that of the American Dream, a mythical text.

The first four studies dealing with interactions between novels are followed by a paper foocusing on intertextual parallels between the book of Exodus and Ignazio Silone's *Fontamara*. The *cafoni's* (peasants') stuggle evokes tribulations of the Hebrews in ancient Egypt. Superimposition of an ancient text upon a modern social problem blots out time distinctions and raises the conflict to a universal structure.

In the next article the volume moves from prose to poetry, but emphasis on self-consciousness reappears as does reference to biblical myths. Anita Hart studies intertextual echoes in José Angel Valente's poems on poetry and language. These references to works of some major poets (Eliot, Mallarmé, Hölderlin, and others) point to the quest for a universal creative principle which is synonymous with a search for the sacred. References to the Bible consequently become relevant.

The next two articles provide a transition from the written to the visual, since they deal with the adaptation of novels to the screen. It is therefore not surprising that Mary Lawlor's essay "Placing Source in *Greed* and *McTeague*" focuses on the central metaphor of gold, a forceful visual symbol. The extensive use and concentration on such a powerful allegory engenders self-consciousness in both narratives which contradicts the effort toward a "realistic" depiction of the West in the novel and the film.

Realism or rather neo-realism in Vittorio DeSica's *Bicycle Thieves* is the topic of Gerard Molyneaux's piece. This time the intertextual conflict derives from combining the novel's vision of a struggling family with the mythic-romantic style of Hollywood in the forties. Molyneaux concludes that the "classical" Hollywood tradition juxtaposed with the sad realities of post-war Italy "make the neo-realistic whole of the film all the more poignant and persuasive."

Another step in the progression toward pure visual studies is Bruce Fleming's "Pictures of Pictures: Two Film Script Versions of Eisenstein's *Potemkin*." While still in the realm of the written text, film scripts can be an intermediate medium between prose fiction and cinema. As for Molyneaux, the representation of reality is again at issue here. Fleming posits that reading film scripts engenders in the mind a "reality effect" in the absence of seeing the film. In a like manner, "the other text" (the film) also creates a vision of reality in the absence of the outside world. "Reading" the Potemkin incident depends upon an interpretation of interactions between texts in different media.

While Fleming analyzes two generic readings of a "historical" incident, the next paper discusses the intertwining of two or more genres within the same film. As in other papers in this volume, Knee once more points out the relationship between intertextuality and self-consciousness. He states that "when differing sets of conventions are forced together, each one becomes foregrounded (or 'marked') to a degree it would not be otherwise." In *Billy the Kid vs. Dracula*, in-jokes about other generic texts are frequent. This interplay leads to an understanding of intergeneric dynamics, important for the appreciation of so many postmodern films.

The last study of E. W. White exemplifies the combination and interaction of various texts which modify the perception of a single image. The article deals with a painting, *Benches*, by Tom Phillips. White's reading of this multimedia work (which includes postcards, painting, collage, weaving, and music) resulted from a viewing at the Tate Gallery in London. It is obvious that every time a work such as this is moved and necessarily reorganized, new readings will occur. In his combinatory approach to aesthetics, Phillips uses components which already contain mixtures of media (images and words). In any case, as we have seen for cinema, the written word is always present in one form or the other (either integrated with the picture or as commentary). The volume, while concluding with a visual study, therefore constantly points to the play within the intertext.

NOTES

[1]Roland Barthes, "Theory of the Text," in *Untying the Text*, ed. Robert Young, trans. Ian McLeod (New York: Routledge and Kegan Paul, 1981) 33.

[2]Mikhaïl Bakhtin, T*he Dialogic Imagination: Four Essays*, ed. Michael Holquist, trans. Caryl Emerson and Michael Holquist (Austin: Univ. of Texas Press, 1981) 292.

[3]Julia Kristeva, "Word, Dialogue and Novel," in *Desire in Language*, ed. Leon S. Oudiez, trans. Thomas Gora, Alice Jardine and Leon Roudiez (New York: Columbia University Press, 1980) 66.

[4]Michel Foucault, "Réponse au Cercle d'Epistémologie," *Cahiers pour l'Analyse* IX (1968) 14.

[5]Barthes, 41.

2. STARTING WITH DOSTOEVSKY'S DOUBLE: BAKHTIN AND NABOKOV AS INTERTEXTUALISTS

John Burt Foster, Jr.

MIKHAIL BAKHTIN (1895-1975) and Vladimir Nabokov (1899-1977) are natural counterparts as intertextualists. Both of them were Russians who came of age during the futurist and formalist challenges to symbolism, in the years of war and revolution from 1914 to 1925. From then until the late 1930s, despite the massive constraints on Soviet culture or the difficulties of exile, they succeeded in launching major careers as Russian-language writers. But only in the later 1950s did their full importance become known outside relatively small circles; and by the late 1960s Bakhtin and Nabokov had gained international recognition, one as a literary and cultural theorist and the other as a practitioner of modern fiction.

With both of them this belated acknowledgment included intense interest in their treatment of intertextuality. In 1967, in France, when Julia Kristeva reviewed Bakhtin's books on Dostoevsky and Rabelais, she coined the very term (441) so as to give a new, text-oriented meaning to what Bakhtin had called "double-voiced discourse," "dialogue," or "polyphony." This usage has since been seconded by Todorov in his book on Bakhtin's dialogic principle. Three years after Kristeva's review, in an equivalent landmark event in United States, Alfred Appel brought out the *Annotated Lolita,* which documented Nabokov's elaborate use of such intertextual practices as allusion, citation, and parody, practices which Appel conceptualized under the rubrics of literary gamesmanship and self-conscious or involuted narration. These important appropriations of Bakhtin and Nabokov take us, however, quite far from the special cultural milieu within which they first emerged as intertextualists. This essay proposes to consider one key element from this Russian background, not because I mean to discount later developments among French structuralists or American postmodernists, but because Bakhtin's and Nabokov's shared point of departure will point up important differences in their approaches to intertextuality.

To understand their positions, we should compare two works originally published quite early in their careers and then reissued in the sixties with significant revisions.[1] I am thinking of Bakhtin's 1929 Dostoevsky book now known as *Problems of Dostoevsky's Poetics* and of Nabokov's 1934 novel *Despair* with its Dostoevsky parodies and polemics. Bakhtin, of course, strongly admires Dostoevsky, and postulates an historical narrative of canon formation which would make him the great originator of the polyphonic novel; this new form of writing, though anticipated by various tendencies among the ancients, had finally vindicated the claims of prose fiction over the traditional classical genres. But Nabokov dismisses Dostoevsky, "our national expert in soul ague and the aberrations of human self-respect" as he is called at one point in *Despair* (74). And as an alternative to the Dostoevsky cult which swept modern audiences in the early twentieth century, Nabokov would later propose a more recent but internationally less prominent Russian writer, the symbolist Andrei Bely.

In making this substitution Nabokov did not have Bakhtin's remarkable long view of the novel reaching back to classical antiquity, and even in modern fiction he tends to dismiss or overlook such writers as Mann, Faulkner, and Woolf, all of whom experimented with multiple perspectives in a manner consistent with Bakhtinian polyphony. On the other hand, Bakhtin himself did not seem to know of these modern writers when he developed his theories, and even the 1963 version of his Dostoevsky book adds only a few hasty references to Mann. Nabokov's own preferences further highlight Bakhtin's relative ignorance of twentieth-century fiction. For he associates Bely with another line of novelists which began with Flaubert, Dostoevsky's exact contemporary in France, and led up to Proust, Joyce, and Kafka;[2] but when Bakhtin touches on the same contrast, he can only cite at second hand a congenially worded critique of the "epopee of the Flaubert school, cut from a single piece, polished and monolithic" (15). He shows none of Nabokov's detailed knowledge of all four novelists, nor is it even clear that he sees Proust, Joyce, and Kafka as followers of Flaubert.

Despite the great differences between these two approaches to fiction, the young Dostoevsky's 1846 novella *The Double* pinpoints an important area of convergence between Bakhtin and Nabokov which does not depend on any mutual influence but on their shared background as Russians steeped in Russian literature. In this story, which ingeniously reworks motifs from his immediate predecessor Gogol, Dostoevsky continued the essentially parodistic strategy he had used in beginning his career with *Poor Folk*, which had also drawn on Gogol. Even contemporary critics had noticed the link, but among Russian formalists when Bakhtin and Nabokov came of age, Dostoevsky's initial recoil from Gogol led far beyond a traditional concern for sources or parallels. Thus Tynyanov, in his ambitious 1921 essay "Dostoevsky and Gogol: Toward a Theory of Parody," treated *The Double* as an epitome of the zig-zag dynamics of literary history, where each generation turns against its immediate predecessor. And later in the twenties Vinogradov and Bem offered more detailed readings which further clarified the stylistic and polemical aspects of the relationship.[3]

11

For Bakhtin and Nabokov the formalists' fascination with Dostoevsky's intertextual link to Gogol would provide a shared point of departure for their own distinctive approaches. Thus when I speak in my title of "starting with *The Double*," I am making the historical point that this work had an important place in their Russian heritage as they began their careers. But once we look at their two books in more detail, we shall see that they "start" with *The Double* in an important conceptual sense as well. Both Bakhtin and Nabokov refer back to Dostoevsky's novella as if it were a basic model, or a major presupposition for their own approaches.

Bakhtin first mentions *The Double* in the second chapter of his Dostoevsky book, right as he begins expounding his master-concept, the dialogical principle, by taking up the issue of narrator-character relations, especially the relative independence of the hero with respect to the author. Offering yet another interpretation of Dostoevsky's recoil from Gogol, he stresses its significance as a paradigmatic break with monologically conceived fiction; thus he argues that the young Dostoevsky "carried out, as it were, a small-scale Copernican revolution when he took what had been [in Gogol] a firm and finalizing authorial definition" (49). But only in Bakhtin's fifth and final chapter, which deals with discourse and the prospects for a metalinguistic approach to literature, does he discuss *The Double* in depth. At this point he advances high claims for its priority, holding that here dialogism appears "with a sharpness and clarity not found in any other work of Dostoevsky's." The basic principle therefore reveals itself with "extraordinary boldness and consistency, carried to their conceptual limits" (211).

As Bakhtin develops this approach, however, he tends to highlight only the interaction of voices within the novella. Though he eventually notes the double-voiced discourse created by the numerous links with Gogol, he begins elsewhere, with a detailed discussion of the hero Golyadkin's split personality. This split, he argues, generates an inner dialogue within the character which oscillates disconcertingly between

12

self-effacement and boldness. Ultimately, with the appearance of Golyadkin's double, the dialogue becomes delusional, with the double's hyperbolical self-assertiveness balancing the original Golyadkin's timidity. As the story develops, moreover, this split spreads even to the narrator, whose condescending, even jeering tone toward the hero mimics the attitude of the double.

For Bakhtin, clearly, the Gogol parody has become just one instance of a more general novelistic process of interaction with what he calls "the word of another." Hence, in a famous chart (199) displaying the many linguistic and literary situations where such interaction takes place, he places parody with phenomena ranging from the stylistic tone of single words to broad questions of irony and authorial perspective. And as the Golyadkin analysis shows, by this point dialogism includes internal relationships which could meaningfully be called intertextual only if we divide *The Double* into mini-texts. Kristeva, in her review, obliquely acknowledges this terminological slippage. For even as she reconceives Bakhtinian dialogism in terms of intertextuality, she makes a distinction between horizontal and vertical dimensions of the intertextual. She then indicates that only the vertical refers to a text's orientation toward previous and contemporary bodies of writing; while the horizontal involves what she calls "the writing subject and its addressee," terms which seem to cover (among other possibilities) the narrator/character relations emphasized by Bakhtin's analysis of *The Double* (440). But when Kristeva goes on to say that "every text is built as a mosaic of citations, every text is the absorption and transformation of another text" (440-41), she has in effect disregarded her own distinction. Vertical intertextuality comes to stand for the whole phenomenon, thereby obscuring the richness of Bakhtin's treatment of *The Double*, since although he mentions its striking "vertical" relation to Gogol, he does not in fact focus on this more narrowly intertextual issue.

Yet within Bakhtin's treatment of Dostoevsky's entire career, this vertical intertextuality receives powerful reinforcement from another direction when he discusses the major works beginning with *Notes from Underground*. For in his third chapter, on the status of the idea in Dostoevsky's work (78), he has already told us that Golyadkin laid the groundwork for the polyphonic novels of Dostoevsky's major phase. In dealing with these works, Bakhtin again expands his interest in "the word of another," to cover the interacting ideological positions of characters like Raskolnikov in relation to Sonya, Svidrigailov, and the examining magistrate Porfiry Petrovich, or of the Karamazov brothers taken as a group. And ideologies, even more than parodies of a specific author, represent discourse systems from outside a work which nonetheless exert pressure on it. The basic trend of Bakhtin's approach is thus to move from the young Dostoevsky the parodist toward the mature Dostoevsky the novelist of sharply distinguished socio-cultural positions. He ends up canonizing the ideological "pro and contra" of the major novels.

With Nabokov, despite his emphatic dislike for Dostoevsky, it is clear that he agreed about the importance of *The Double*. In his university lectures on the Russian novel, given in later 1940s and the 1950s, he singled out Dostoevsky's novella as "the very best thing he ever wrote" and "a perfect work of art" (*Lectures on Russian Lit*, 104). But Nabokov realizes that he is arguing a minority position. Most readers admired Dostoevsky as a great prophet, he concedes, and their single-minded pursuit of edifying messages kept them from appreciating *The Double*'s "imitation of Gogol" that was "at times almost a parody." Nabokov would also praise the novella's elaborate expressiveness as "almost Joycean," thus summoning up his way of reading *Ulysses*. In that novel he strongly endorsed Joyce's handling of "the prism of a parody," most notably in the "Nausicaa" episode, which "manages to build up something real—pathos, pity, compassion—out of the dead formulas he parodies" (*Lectures on Lit*, 289, 347). Alone among Dostoevsky's works, then, *The Double* could become the model for one of Nabokov's characteristic aims as a novelist, an aim which Appel would later stress in the *Annotated Lolita*. In his introduction

14

(liii), Appel aligns his intertextual approach with a programmatic statement in Nabokov's first English novel *The Real Life of Sebastian Knight,* where parody is envisioned "as a kind of springboard for leaping into the highest region of serious emotion" (91). In effect Nabokov has tailored the formalist view of Dostoevsky to his own project of creative parody, thereby turning a scholarly discussion into a manifesto for one trend in twentieth-century writing.

His brilliant novel *Despair* is an early example of this parodistic method. It is the story of Herman Karlovich, an unsuccessful chocolate merchant who tries to devise a crime whose perfection would rival art. After meeting a tramp named Felix whom he believes resembles him exactly, Herman conceives the idea of murdering him and then switching identities so that the death will seem his own and his wife can collect the insurance money. The idea is far from original; and when Nabokov informs us as early as the second page that Herman had read over a thousand books while in internment during World War I, he suggests the work's intertextual range in the vertical, more classical sense of the term. Nabokov's very choice of names suggests something of the novel's cross-cultural scope: if Herman himself recalls the German hero of Pushkin's "Queen of Spades," Felix more fleetingly evokes certain parallels with Thomas Mann's confidence man Felix Krull. And Herman's car—a delightful little Icarus, he tells us—accurately gauges his artistic pretensions alongside Joyce's Stephen Dedalus.

Despite this breadth of allusion, however, Dostoevsky is clearly a dominant intertextual presence, as Herman indicates when he looks over his manuscript account of the murder and weighs possible titles:

> What amazed me was the absence of title on the first leaf: for assuredly I had at one time invented a title, something beginning with "Memoirs of a"—of a what? I could not remember; and, anyway, "Memoirs" seemed dreadfully dull and commonplace. What should I call my book then? "The Double"? but Russian literature possessed one already.

15

"Crime and Pun"? Not bad—a little crude, though. "The
Mirror"? "Portrait of the Artist in a Mirror"? (169)

We spot another reference to Joyce, of course; while "Memoirs," which
corresponds to the Russian word "zapinski" in the original, evokes
many works including "Zapiski Sumasshedshego" and "Zapiski
Okhotnika," Gogol's "Diary of a Madman" and Turgenev's
"Sportsman's Sketches." But Herman's reflections make no fewer than
four references to Dostoevsky, the author of *Notes from the House of
the Dead* and *Notes from Underground*, both of them "Zapiski," along
with the more obvious *Crime and Punishment* and *The Double*.

Simply listing the allusions in this passage does not, however, do
justice to the underlying process of intertextual absorption and
transformation, which is directed by a specific attitude toward
Dostoevsky. By this point readers realize that Herman, like his
namesake in Pushkin, is mad; so among the many Zapiski in Russian
literature, Gogol's "Diary of a Madman" has priority. Herman's
avoidance of this title leads him to think of *The Double* instead, so in
effect he retraces the young Dostoevsky's reaction against Gogol; but at
this stage in Russian letters, Herman dimly realizes, Dostoevsky has
forestalled this move, and so he suggests the more polemical title of
Crime and Pun. This ingenious proposal, where the parodic play with a
predecessor and Herman's sense of Felix as a visual pun on himself
recall *The Double* but where the title itself points up the echoes between
Herman's murder-plot and Raskolnikov's crime, comes closer to the
basic donnee of *Despair*. Moreover, by turning *The Double*'s anti-
Gogolian technique of parody against its own inventor, it also succeeds
in capturing Nabokov's complex attitude toward Dostoevsky, which
mingles respect for that novella with general detestation. The Joyce
reference, finally, acknowledges the contribution of early twentieth-
century modernism to this rewriting of Dostoevsky.

Despair contains many small-scale parodic confrontations with
Dostoevsky, of the kind Bakhtin would call microdialogues. One near
the beginning of the novel is particularly illuminating, since it helps

show how Nabokov justified his distaste for the ideological dimension in the later Dostoevsky. Herman has just started writing the book; and after extravagant praise for his own gifts as an author, he breaks off to make a self-serving remark: "At this point I should have compared the breaker of the law which makes such a fuss over a little spilled blood, with a poet or stage performer" (13). Stylistically, this microdialogue evokes the underground man's behavior as a first-person narrator, as he constantly interrupts his notes with self-conscious asides to the reader. Intellectually, however, it recalls Raskolnikov's famous article on crime, which began by praising Kepler and Newton as creative "lawbreakers," then extended the analogy to Napoleonic leaders who did not hesitate to act ruthlessly, and finally used their example to justify murder by certain extraordinary individuals.[4]

Nabokov's rewriting of these two Dostoevsky passages tellingly eliminates their ideological element. The underground man's self-conscious asides, which registered an intuitive protest against simplistic utilitarian thought, are converted into an artistic judgment. For they show that Herman cannot write as effortlessly and compellingly as he claims, therefore implying that he is a creative failure. As a result his Raskolnikov-like argument for murder on the basis of artistic genius falls to pieces, and this discrepancy between his claims and reality becomes even clearer when Herman examines his true feelings while writing:

> And again there would grow in me that prickly feeling, that unendurable twitter . . . and my will lay limp in an empty world. . . . No, these are not the throes of creation . . . but something quite different (15).

Nabokov, in short, has restored the sharp distinction between creativity and criminality, which had been obscured by Raskolnikov's quick glide from lawbreaking in the realm of scientific hypotheses to gratuitous acts of murder.

Twenty years later, in Nabokov's lectures on Russian fiction, he was still arguing with this passage in *Crime and Punishment*. Its "fast transition" from Newton to Napoleon, he would insist, is "worth a more detailed psychological analysis than Dostoevski, in his hurry, can afford to make" (*Lectures on Russian Lit*, 114). If pressed, Nabokov would have said his basic criteria at this point were aesthetic, not simply because he is concerned with Dostoevsky's techniques as a writer but also because he appeals to broader artistic issues that include both creativity in general and a stubborn fidelity to the individual case. When Dostoevsky the ideologue used Raskolnikov's article to score a point against scientific rationalism, he overlooked what Kepler and Newton meant in themselves, and thereby misrepresented their particular creative achievement. Nabokov thus rejects what Bakhtin, in commenting on this very passage from *Crime and Punishment*, had held was the source of Dostoevsky's greatness—the power of bringing together "ideas and worldviews, which in real life were absolutely estranged and deaf to one another" (91). From Nabokov's aesthetic perspective, however, this power boiled down to polemical exaggeration and a refusal to consider the elementary distinction between creativity and criminality.

As an intertextualist, Nabokov consciously exploits the dialogic principle of defining one's position against the utterances of others. And his art of parody, which received its first major impetus in *Despair*, is a fictional equivalent for that aspect of Bakhtinian theory devoted to Dostoevsky's reworkings of Gogol. But, though Nabokov may be more alert to modernist experiments in fiction, he lacks Bakhtin's power of theoretical generalization, and so he fails to see parody's relation to more basic interactive processes throughout discourse. Nabokov diverges even more from Bakhtin when he insists, in the wake of Flaubert and others, that novels should belong to an aesthetic realm apart from ideology. As a result he can dismiss Dostoevsky's major phase because its emphasis on conflicting ideas and values appeared to neglect art in favor of biased or caricatured thoughts. But Bakhtin, in affirming the later Dostoevsky, takes a sharply contrasting viewpoint. Thus in "Discourse in the Novel," written several years after his Dostoevsky book, he can define fiction as the genre "least susceptible to aestheticism" by virtue of "being a dialogized representation of an ideologically freighted discourse" (333).

Yet despite Bakhtin's and Nabokov's differing positions on ideology and art, on theory and practice, or on Dostoevsky's very place in modern fiction, their approaches to intertextuality did emerge from a shared setting. And as they relate back in their separate ways to Dostoevsky's *Double*, which was itself a transposition of Gogol, they epitomize one additional property of intertextuality as a concept. When these textual chains are analyzed in their own right, they have a tendency to reveal processes of dispersion, or what Jonathan Culler has called "perspectives of unmasterable series" (111), within the ongoing work of cultural transmission.

NOTES

[1]In this essay I shall normally refer to the final revised editions of both works, though on occasion I shall take account of the original versions. The full extent of Bakhtin's and Nabokov's changes, though undoubtedly interesting, cannot be studied here.

[2]On Bely in relations to Joyce, Proust, and Kafka, see *Strong Opinions*, p. 57. On Flaubert's relation to these three early twentieth-century masters, see *Lectures on Literature*, pp. 147, 256.

[3]All of these formalist essays have been conveniently collected and translated into English by Pricilla Meyer and Stephen Rudy.

[4]Raskolnikov explains this theory in *Crime and Punishment*, Part III, Chapter 5.

WORKS CITED

Bakhtin, Mikhail. "Discourse in the Novel." In *The Dialogic Imagination*. Ed. Michael Holquist. Trans. Caryl Emerson and Michael Holquist. Austin: Univ. of Texas Press, 1981.

———. *Problems of Dostoevsky's Poetics*. Ed. and trans. Caryl Emerson. Introd. Wayne C. Booth. Minneapolis: Univ. of Minnesota Press, 1984.

Culler, Jonathan. "Presupposition and Intertextuality." In *The Pursuit of Signs—Semiotics, Literature, Deconstruction*. Ithaca NY: Cornell Univ. Press, 1981: 100-118.

Kristeva, Julia. "Bakhtine, le mot, le dialogue et le roman." *Critique* 23 (1967): 438-65.

Meyer, Pricilla and Rudy, Stephen, eds. *Dostoevsky and Gogol: Texts and Criticism*. Ann Arbor MI: Ardis, 1979.

Nobokov, Vladimir. *The Annotated Lolita*. Ed., Introd., and Annotated by Alfred Appel. New York: McGraw-Hill, 1970.

———. *Despair*. Trans. Dmitri Nabokov with revisions by Vladimir Nabokov. New York: G.P. Putnam's, 1966.

———. *Lectures on Literature*. Introd. John Updike. Ed. Fredson Bowers. New York: Harcourt Brace Jovanovich, 1980.

———. *Lectures on Russian Literature*. Ed. and Introd. Fredson Bowers. New York: Harcourt Bracc Jovanovich, 1981.

———. *The Real Life of Sebastian Knight*. Norfolk CT: New Directions, 1941.

———. *Strong Opinions*. New York: McGraw-Hill. 1973.

Todorov, Tzvetan. *Mikhail Bakhtin: the Dialogic Principle*. Trans. Wlad Godzich. Minneapolis: Univ. of Minnesota Press, 1984.

3. A CHARACTER'S INDICTMENT OF AUTHORIAL SUBTERFUGE: THE PARODY OF TEXTS IN ROBERTO G. FERNANDEZ'S FICTION

Jorge Febles

TO DATE, ROBERTO G. FERNANDEZ has authored three amorphous novels of varying lengths. *La vida es un special $.75* (1981) and *La montaña rusa* (1985) are linguistic hybrids in which an essentially neutral Spanish coexists with dialectal or idiolectic variants, as well as with English and a heterogeneous Spanglish. However, his latest book *Raining Backwards* (1988), is written almost entirely in English, a dominant language that—within the text—devours in symbolically genocidal fashion a minority tongue: Spanish. Notwithstanding scriptural contrasts generated by this salient distinction, all three works embrace a similar Menippean model. They are polyphonic, multi-generic, contradictory, heteroglot constructs whose objective is grotesquely to demythologize a particular social group, the Cuban-American community established in Miami.[1] By formulating a microcosm that constitutes the laughing double of its referent, Fernández seeks to anathematize in jest a collectivity rhetorically and

21

ideologically immersed in the past, although it has adapted or conformed to *foreign* tenets that exact at times the denial, at times the transformation, of such unifying features as language, traditions, mores, even that nostalgia inherent to a learned racial memory. Hence, these narratives seem historically dynamic and politically confrontational. Degrading a conservative world view characterized by paranoid instability, they integrate one unfinished parody, one forever incomplete volume where death implies renewal but not radical change, where time is elastic, where unharmonious voices clash only so that the uttered words (devoid of signification) may disappear into nothingness.

Latent in this carnivalesque system is an intertextuality that diversifies parodic impact. For the purpose of illuminating its intrinsic ambiguity, I have ventured to read Fernández's novels from the perspective of the recurrent personage: eccentric Eloy de los Reyes, a Funes-like entity consumed by remembrances of unexperienced realities. In order to defend himself from the real author's denigrating discourse, he assumes synecdochically the mocked society's aggregate voice, reiterating—I trust—an essential narrative tone. Serendipitously and gratuitously aged to verbalize thoughts more profound than those associated with his previous fictional persona, this peculiar being affects a censorious pose to betray the writer's inventive dependence upon whole or fragmentary pre-texts. In short, I have hijacked Eloy's language and point of view—perhaps redefined or even adulterated them—to expand tongue-in-cheek, of course, the perceivable dialogic squabble between creature and creator. The latter's predisposition to chastise the former permits focusing naively on such palpable matters as poetic intention, character development, and intertextual components. Through his exposé, Eloy will confirm instead the sophisticated effectiveness of authorial technique.

I hope you remember, Roberto (or should I call you Mr. Fernández, as becomes a novelist, or maybe Dr. Fernández, bilingually

22

trained educator of bilinguals, as suggests the pedant who will interrupt me all too often with bothersome clarifications, with notes upon notes that lead nowhere), I hope you remember what I, Eloy de los Reyes, the repeatable, the never-forgotten one, told that brainless psychiatrist whom you forced me to consult in *La vida es un special $.75* when I was older (for then indeed I was much older than now, in *Raining Backwards,* where—nasty trickster who alters facts like a punk rocker changes hair styles and coloring—you've brought me to re-encounter puberty, as if it wasn't hard enough the first time around). Anyhow, I'll remind you just in case by paraphrasing like you would, yes, like you would, those phrases which I uttered in defeat, aware already of your wicked intentions, worried, as I made plain, about my lack of psychological progression. I complained to the seed-casting witch doctor (was he a relative of yours?) that it was perfectly justifiable for others to be empty vacuum cleaners, but—this is a quote—"I had been promised the opportunity to develop,"[2] to become somebody different, and by this time it seemed unfeasible. Was I condemned to be another mere airhead, a hollow mannequin, a God-forsaken dummy trapped in my nostalgia maze, wearing an outfit proper for some half-baked Siboney Indian, or, naked, trying to rediscover paradise in my private Varadero, my little bathtub beach built with ground sand, a good portable heater, an electric fan, and hard tap water aptly dyed to resemble Germán García's aquamarine sea of illusions?[3] I voiced my fear of being termed "a character of little depth,"[4] and now, seven years later, I ask: Were my concerns—addressed to you—addressed by you? Was I allowed to evolve logically? Did I change, for instance, in *La montaña rusa,* in that Russian mountain-turned-rollercoaster where I worshipped Lola, my mythical chorus girl, my filmed queen, while still reposing (older than before) in that private Varadero, drowning my longing with daiquiris prepared in the bathroom sink, my longing caused by memories so vivid that Barry Manilow could set them to music if he hasn't already?[5] But after tantalizing readers with my tale, after leading them and me to think I would advance, talk further, become fuller and more complex, you removed me from the pages, you had me fly, like Matías Pérez, in search of inconsistent clouds.[6] The ultimate affront, however, is this last one of *Raining Backwards,* where you again use me (abuse me seems a better term) to introduce the books, transforming me into some twerpy teeny-bopper who wastes his time rubbing a sixty-year old lecher's wrinkled back, for Christ's sake. Even worse: You imply through her words that I copied my story, my dream, my very own nostalgia from her. She steals my beach (the bitch) and lies in it and prides herself on being the original architect. Why does she swipe my eyes, my mind, I ask? It's as if you—the controller, the amoral arbiter—assumed that anyone's life is everyone's life, that individual recollections are universal. Only the voices change, and the approaches to experiences. That is why now, seeking a break, asking for regeneration as well as development in what must inevitably come, I rob a fool's typewriter to indict you, publicly showing (and in English) that you're nothing but a word thief, that you borrow mercilessly from songs, poems, novels, letters, essays, hell, even from "Tío Chaguito," "Abuela Cuca," "Papá Pototo," all those gentle people whom you meet walking along Eighth Street.[7] I'll demonstrate that when one looks for you in your stories, you are nowhere to be found: You are no voice, you have no voice, you are nothing but a huge smirk poking fun at the world. Which makes me feel a little more secure already, for I'm fixed in words and memory while you are merely oblivion. (*Pedantic Intervention Number 1:* Bakhtin writes: "In the comic world there is nothing for memory to do. One ridicules in order to forget.")[8]

Let's focus on distorted songs. I mean, is there a character in your books who, when talking, does not incorporate into his speech in bizarre manner fragments of popular *boleros, guarachas, sones,* rock ballads, good honest tunes that, for some reason, become strange and make those who quote them appear strange? (*Pedantic Intervention Number 2:* In Fernández's three narratives, personages frequently cite, as intrinsic parts of their individual discourse, portions of musical compositions whose ideological triteness—demythologized by context, by transparent "intonational quotation marks"[9] which enclose them—magnify parodic effect. Signifiers of stereotypical bourgeois attitudes toward country, love, beauty, sex, their degradation promotes uproarious laughter.) I'll rudely remind you by noting some examples. There is pop psychologist Helen Kings, Ann Landers think-alike, romantic plagiarist (or are you the plagiarist?) who mimicked Julio Iglesias' plaintive chants in her response to grieving customer Connie: "When you lose, when you finally realize it, time does not allow you to return."[10] This is the selfsame letter where before she had echoed José Luis Perales, singing on paper: "What is he like? And where did he fall in love with you?"[11] How about that vulgar Bilingual Mockingbird who, in *La montaña rusa,* intones obscene lyrics that I won't repeat because, unlike you, I'm decent and don't dare offend my cultured readers, my ingenuous audience. They must skim your brutal book to be offended. And through these songs that any ten-year-old Cuban boy knew by heart the dirty feathered friend obtained a radio program? What does that pretend to state about our community? Why should you degrade it so? In *La montaña rusa* as well, Keith Rodríguez (incestuous pervert, cocaine vender, evil rebel) lied to his sister Connie that a Cuban philosopher had once said to Nietzsche (much like skinny Ñico Membiela would serenade through his melodious nose): "I only ask of you one favor if you are not opposed. Be a little less proud and have more patience. Beauty is an illusion that soon fades. Eternal beauty is in the soul."[12] Now, in *Raining Backwards,* we undress verbally in our adoptive language, anglicized beings whose speech often patterns itself after American songs. For example, Connie Rodríquez (she of "Bang, bang, choo-choo train, c'mon Dolphins, do your thing!"[13] fame) consults Dr. Helen Kings about a note from her murderous boyfriend Bill Cloonan where—imitating Billy Joel—he begged to be given one more chance, to be told that her sweet love hadn't died. "Dr. Kings"—continues the eager but foiled cheerleader, the soon-to-be gruesomely slaughtered football worshipper—"He's got a way about him and I just don't know what it is!" (*RB* 61) During an ensuing rapturous encounter, while Bill, the foul blond, seductively declaims sweet rhymes by Bécquer, dark, sensuous Connie evokes funky Mel Carter. "Hold me. Kiss me. Thrill me" (*RB* 65) she demands. What's the point? Why does she, why do so many of us echo such songs? It's certainly not because, having a natural sense of rhythm, our ideas are unavoidably linked to music. So it may be that you—background snickerer, devil not angel—ill-use temporarily appropriated tongues, poke fun at characters, in other words, while ridiculing time-tested pop tunes, holy words. Admit it: Sometimes you're a real jerk.

Among the most hateful things I've discovered parading through your fictions, Mr. Fernández, is a propensity to put down commonly-held beliefs, usual behavior, respected customs, even patriotic zeal. It's accomplished like this: You have us move around in a wide-open society where anything goes, where nothing is crazy or sacred because all that's sacred is crazy, where death is funny and love is only sex. (*Pedantic Intervention Number 3:* such generalized carnivalesque atmosphere—irreverent, grotesque, anarchically free—intimates that the three novels form a continuum focused on one objective or final image: To depict "the gay funeral of a dying era.")[14] In our abnormal world, deprived of seriousness, each standard notion appears scornful, exaggerated, unnatural. For example, we utter opinions that you've picked up—robbed is more precise—from all kinds of persons (friends, relatives, strangers, poor suckers every one, who had no inkling you were xeroxing their brains). In our mouths these ideas—because of the surroundings that you've manufactured for us and because of the slightly extravagant manner in which we tend to express them—become somewhat silly, which (I assume) is what gives you that air of superiority you exhibit from afar. It must make you feel very good, Mr. Fernández, to think of me as a bad case of memorial herpes, consumed by peculiar habits and prone to verbal diarrhea. Or to compare yourself with old Domingo, the Zeppelin man, whom you exposed to public derision by jotting down some of his nostalgic overstatements. Remember when—complaining about American eggs—he maintained that Cuban hens used to lay hard-shelled and red-yolked ones as big as baseballs, so big in fact that frequently it was necessary to extract them by caesarean section? Or when he argued that in my beloved (your forsaken) island there was once a blimp much larger than those abominable Good Year monstrosities, so large, actually, that it would cause partial eclipses of the Sun? You, always distant, calculating, measured, I imagine, in your political rhetoric, must have thought it a riot to transcribe Apolinar del Rato's impassioned essay, which earned him first prize in the artistic contest sponsored by the Cuban-American Alliance for Freedom and Democracy and for the Prevention of Communism and the Preservation of Cultural Principles and Biculturalism. He wrote in that anti-Leninist *pièce de résistence:*

> Communism is bad, it's the worse thing there is. Communism screwed up the world. . . . Communists steal children and suck their blood and wash their brains. Communism is a great danger for the United States and Americans do not realize it because they eat shit and Kennedy and Roosevelt were communists. . . . Many communists are queers. If I begin to put down the names of communist faggots, the list would reach the South Pole.[15]

His argumentation may sound a mite far-fetched but, after all, isn't it based upon facts proven by our communal experience? Doesn't it conform at heart to our (perhaps not yours, conveniently hidden cad, undercover consciousness) general beliefs? We are not a bunch of hysterics; we are doleful victims of the Red Plague. (*Pedantic Intervention Number 4:* Technically, then, in Fernández's narratives characters often usurp and grotesquely distort a *real* rhetoric illustrative of shared dogmas. Their voices reproduce *foreign* texts made humorous through hyperbole, profanity, erroneous word usage,

27

and so forth. Given the novels' parodic nature, these are demythologized further because they dialogue with an implied author who, simply by being removed, represents sanity within the *mad, mad world.*) I must mention, in passing, that many Americans also people your books, repeating frequently popular credos that become bizarre within the paradise you've build for us. Although the Tongue Brigade (offshoot of the English-Only Movement) is not very much to my liking for obvious reasons, there was no need to confuse their sincere goals by including in *Raining Backwards* that meeting of a radical fringe where someone advocated giving a *final solution* to the Cuban-American problem. Wait until ex-Senator Hayakawa finds out about this. His followers are going to make you doggie-paddle to the Soviet Union.

Let's get down to the nitty-gritty, to the most embarrassing comments I can express about your writings. Naïve, chaste, insecure though you may want me, Master Fernández, I've read a couple of books, enough in fact to note that, as a matter of course, others' fine works appear reflected in your own. When they are transposed to their new habitat, elegant phrases, well-formulated rhymes, complex ideas seem out-of-context, weird, malformed. And this you manage— remote puppeteer, absurd ventriloquist—in cynical and cowardly fashion. Rather than face up to your crimes at least impersonally, you force us to become desecrators by filling our mouths with personal versions of famous authors' words when the moment is not right, when whatever we say will sound nonsensical to the uninvolved reader, especially if we put it in English. (*Pedantic Intervention Number 5:* What Bakhtin has affirmed about another genre, the Latin *parodia sacra,* pertains within reason to these narratives, particularly when one considers their inherent bilingualism. Stated the Soviet critic regarding such "intentional dialogized hybrid," such "dialogue between languages,"

> We have . . . a never-ending folkloric dialogue: the dispute
> between a dismal sacred word and a cheerful folk word. . . .

> Another's sacred word, uttered in a foreign language, is de-
> graded by the accents of vulgar folk languages, and con-
> geals to the point where it becomes a ridiculous image, the
> comic carnival mask of a narrow and joyless pedant, an
> unctuous hypocritical old bigot, a stingy and dried-up
> miser.) (FP 76)

I could go on and on about what you've done to writings by such masters as Gustavo Adolfo Bécquer (whom you'll never meet because he's
not in Hell), Rubén Darío, Pablo Neruda, Mario Vargas Llosa (whose
author's voice you obscenely usurp while aping his Quién mató a
Palomino Molero? in that ludicrous segment of *Raining Backwards,*
entitled "Who killed C.R.?"), Washington Irving, Charles Perrault,
Elizabeth Barrett Browning, Calderón de la Barca, the nameless min-
strel who composed the *Poem of Mío Cid,* Sor Juana Inés de la Cruz,
Christ, even George Washington's field correspondence is jokingly re-
constructed on one occasion. But, to save space, I'll let you a little off
the hook by referring exclusively to the rabid *anti-Martianism* I detect
behind those books which constitute our world. The Apostle's holy
utterances—always sound, profound, enticingly spontaneous—are employed by characters who denigrate them unconsciously with their
own rhetoric, for (as you may be unwilling to admit, depraved pen-
pusher) no one can match Martí's facility of expression, to say nothing
of his virtue, his wisdom, his prudence. To top it all, in *Raining
Backwards* an unidentified mad translator (I pray his name is not
Fernández; or could you possibly have sunk so low?) provides a
mangled version of "Cultivo una rosa blanca," limpid poem,
philosophical beau ideal that should be memorized by every self-
respecting kindergartner. To defame that gem, and then to place it in
Linda Lucía's stained flag-woman's tongue;[16] to have her transform
our hero's name into Joe Marty! Scribe, be damned if you acted
rationally! For the sake of familiarizing others with this atrocity,
with this blasphemous contraption worthy of universal reproach, I
strain my essay through its transcription:

I cultivate a white rose
in July as in January
for the friendly friend
that gives me a frank hand.

And for the cruel one that pulls out
the heart with which I live,
weeds nor nettles
do I cultivate,
I cultivate a white rose. (*RB* 149)

But there are still more opprobrious imitations. In *La montaña rusa*, phrases from one of Martí's famous letters—that gentle epistle to his sister Amelia where, himself wounded by woman, the Apostle asks her to be wary of men's poisonous darts—are enmeshed (with your evil approval, I presume) in lewd Keith Rodríguez's ambiguous message to his *beloved* Connie. Quoting from both texts, I'll show those few hard-nosed readers who yet may doubt me how pure words are tinged with lechery and transformed into inane mutterings of a feeble brain. Martí wrote decorously in his inimitable style, whose intrinsic lyrical qualities I have done my best to convey in this humble translation:

> I have before me, my beautiful Amelia, like a rare jewel which casts a soft, chaste light, your loving letter. In it is found your serene soul, devoid of wickedness, devoid of irrational impatience. In it is found your tender spirit, that overflows from you like the essence of the first May flowers. That is why I want you to guard yourself from violent and treacherous winds, and to seek refuge within while they pass by you: because like birds of prey through the air, those winds traverse the Earth searching for the essence of flowers.[17]

The poet's touching admonition appears crudely deformed when deviant Keith (who awaits, in prison, the Depo-Provera injection that would cure his incestuous appetite) plagiarizes it to soothe despondent Connie. Trapped by intellectual responsibilities, I must reproduce a fragment of the shameful document:

> I have your picture before me, and I keep it like a jewel which casts a soft, chaste light. How I crave a letter from you! At least a couple of hurried lines! I think about your tender spirit that overflows like the essence of the first May flowers. I want you, dear sister, to guard yourself from violent winds, from ignominious slander, because winds are searching for the essence of flowers, my beautiful Madonna lily.[18]

He of the powdery nose and the meandering phallus desecrating holy words! But why go on? My case is proven; the typewriter has burnt in anger.

One last impression before I discard you like a dirty tissue. It seems to me that our cosmos—so flexible, so hectic—may be compared to a Cuban carnival, you know what I mean, a temporary period when everybody wears a mask, when everyone may become another to a conga beat, when serious people—half-drunk, half-mad— will say the strangest things. And I see shadows of authors who have helped you to formulate this chaos in which we laugh agonizingly. I see García Márquez (a gnat attack;[23] the persecuting memory of events to come), and Larra, you cynic, whom you mimic in "Good Night," eccentric version of "El castellano viejo," and Cabrera Infante, pilgrim sound-maker who taught you a mood, a tone. (*Pedantic Intervention Number 6:* Fernández's texts dialogue with a literary tradition which attests the ambivalent nature of laughter and the preeminence of flux, of perpetual crisis.) But that is entirely meaningless, for you are an individual creator now, as distant from them as you are from me, a man who writes truly bilingual books, crazy labyrinths in which I'm lost, in which you are lost. And I— minor character with limited intuition but endowed with an intense desire to become, to question collective reality, to foresee the past while recollecting the future—look for you constantly within our surroundings, finding nothing save an enormous grin. The rest are voices, awkward voices like my own.

NOTES

[1]Critically, this essay is based to a substantial degree on Bakhtinian notions and terminology advanced in the following texts: M.M. Bakhtin, "Epic and Novel: Toward a Methodology for the Study of the Novel" and "From the Prehistory of Novelistic Discourse," *The Dialogic Imagination: Four Essays*, trans. Caryl Emerson and Michael Holquist, ed. Michael Holquist (Austin: University of Texas Press, 1981) 3-40, 41-83; Bakhtin, *Problems of Dostoevsky's Poetics*, trans. and ed. Caryl Emerson (Minneapolis: University of Minnesota Press, 1984); *Bakhtin, Rabelais and His World*, trans. Helene Iswolsky (Bloomington: Indiana University Press, 1984).

[2]Roberto G. Fernández, *La vida es un special $.75* (Miami: Universal, 1981) 41. In Spanish, Eloy says: "A mí se me prometió que se me iba a dar la oportunidad de desarrollarme."

[3]The reference to singer Germán García's interpretation of "Varadero," a pop tune popular in Cuba during the late fifties, constitutes a parodic leif-motiv in Fernández's three novels.

[4]Fernández, *La vida es un special .75*. 41. In Spanish, Eloy says: "Me calificarán de personaje poco profundo."

[5]A mythical abstraction, Eloy's Lola is the same character about whom Barry Manilow sang in his top-forty hit "Copacabana." Hence the binary allusion.

[6]Around the turn of this century, Cuban aviator Matías Pérez disappeared while attempting a balloon flight to Key West. Since then, the expression "he/she flew like Matías Pérez" became part of popular speech. It is used to ridicule someone's sudden exit from any

particular place. In Fernández's novels, references to this semi-legendary character punctuate both their comicality and the folkoric nature of discourse.

[7]Eighth Street constitutes the heart of Miami's Little Havana.

[8]Bakhtin, "Epic and Novel" 23.

[9]Bakhtin, "From the Prehistory" 50.

[10]Fernández, *La montaña rusa* (Houston: Arte Público Press, l985) 85. In Spanish, Dr. Kings quotes Julio Iglesias' hit song "Momentos": "Cuando pierdes, cuando al fin te has dado cuenta, el tiempo no te deja regresar."

[11]Fernández, *La montaña* 85. In Spanish, Dr. Kings quotes a fragment of "&Y cómo es él?," a song by Spanish balladeer José Luis Perales: "&Cómo es él? &En qué lugar se enamoró de ti?"

[12]Fernández, *La montaña* 172. In Spanish, Keith Rodríquez uses some lines from a composition popularized during the l950's by Ñico Membiela, a Cuban singer famous for his nasal twang: "Sólo te pido un favor si no te opones. No seas tan orgulloso y ten más calma. La Belleza . . . es ilusión que pasa. La belleza eterna está en el alma."

[13]Fernández, *Raining Backwards* (Houston: Arte Público Press, l988). 87.

[14]Bakhtin, *Rabelais* 99

[15]Fernández, *La montaña* ll3. In Spanish, Apolinar del Rato writes the following:

> El comunismo es malo, es la cosa más mala que existe. El comunismo jodió al mundo. . . . Los comunistas se llevan a los niños y le (sic) shupan la sangre y les lavan el cerebro. El comunismo en América es un gran peligro y los americanos no se dan cuenta porque ellos son comemierdas y Kennedy y Roosevelt eran comunistas. . . . Muchos de los comunistas son maricones. Si me pongo a escribir los nombres de los comunistas maricones llegaría-se aquí al Polo Sur.

[16]Linda Lucía is a grotesque recurrent character conceived along the lines of what may be termed a folk symbolic archetype. As a young girl, she was outfitted like the Cuban flag and made to wear chains representative of the enslaved nation. This bizarre fictional metaphor is based upon a concrete ceremonial entity. For instance, in January 28, 1988, during Ybor City's (Florida) parade to commemorate José Martí's anniversary, a pretty teenager rode on a float attired precisely in such carnivalesque fashion.

[17]José Martí, "To Amelia Martí," 1888, *La gran enciclopedia martiana*, 14 vols. (Miami: Editorial Martiana, 1978), vol. 5, 382. Eloy translates the following segment:

> Tengo delante de mí, mi hermosa Amelia, como una joya rara y de luz blanda y pura, tu cariñosa carta. Ahí está tu alma serena, sin mancha, sin locas impaciencias. Ahí tu espíritu tierno, que rebosa de ti como la esencia de las primeras flores de mayo. Por eso quiero yo que te guardes de vientos violentos y traidores, y te escondas en ti a verlos pasar: que como las aves de rapiña por los aires, andan los vientos por la tierra en busca de la esencia de las flores.

[18]Fernández, *La montaña* 171. Eloy translates the following segment:

> Delante de mí tengo tu retrato, y lo guardo como una joya rara y de luz blanda y pura. Cómo añoro una carta tuya! Al menos dos borrones y unas letras! Pienso en tu espíritu tierno, que rebosa como la esencia de las primeras flores de mayo. Quiero, querida hermana, que te guardes de vientos violentos, de calumnias ignominiosas, que andan los vientos en busca de la esencia de las flores, mi bella azucena tierna.

[19]The gnats which persecute specific characters in *Raining Backwards* are reminiscent of those yellow butterflies that always ac-

company Mauricio Babilonia in García Márquez's *One Hundred Years of Solitude*.

4. FEDERATED FANCIES: BALZAC'S *LOST ILLUSIONS* AND MELVILLE'S *PIERRE*

Benjamin Sherwood Lawson

MANY MID-NINETEENTH-CENTURY European and American novels trace the careers of young protagonists who set forth into new experience. Somewhat fewer describe the growth and fates of writers and thereby become commentaries on art. Our formulating of these genres of *Bildungsroman* and *Künstlerroman* may force readings and blind us to more specific and perhaps more profound similarities among novels. The books discussed here, for example, completed within ten years of each other, are strikingly akin on many fronts. But they exist together on a deeper level than as depictions of a moment in Western society or of a writer's enlightenment. Pierre's French name is only the initial (and a superficial) point at which Honoré de Balzac's *Lost Illusions* and Herman Melville's *Pierre, or, the Ambiguities* meet.[1]

In general and in particular, *Pierre* (1852) is an unwitting recasting of *Lost Illusions* (1837-43) by way of extensive parallels between the two works in plot, characterization, and theme: the mothers of both Lucien Chardon and Pierre Glendinning are from aristocratic families; portraits of the dead serve as "characters"; the protagonists are writers

37

of both fiction and poetry; their early poems are puerile, flowery, derivative sonnets; settings shift from the provinces to the city (although Balzac classified the novel as a "scene of provincial life"), where a devaluation of self and work occurs, and where public acknowledgment of relationships with women is made possible; misfortune brings each protagonist to reflection and a questioning of naive optimism; references are made to Dante; early companions appear who achieve careers as "poets," which contrast with Lucien's and Pierre's careers; all kinds of publishing are presented as merely trade, as prostitution; repositories of cloistered artistic virtue are described in the Cénacle of Balzac's novel and in "the Apostles" of Melville's; the main characters meet death by suicide, in prison (an event adumbrated in *Lost Illusions* although it occurs in *Splendor and Misery of Courtesans*). Detailed analysis could be made of the significance of each of these similarities.

More central and basic to these novels is the self-reflexivity that stems from their dwelling upon the phenomena of meaning and indeterminacy and of the very substance of writing implements, ink, print, and paper. The books call attention to themselves not only as works of art, with content resulting from the referential transparency of the word, but as opaque objects. Both novels have problematic titles which in no definite way announce a theme. The term "illusions" has multiple implications, could apply to any of several characters, and the whole title contains a redundancy—illusion being not so much a positive ideal as it is any false mental image. Applied to objects, the word may signify a chimera or deception of the eye. The title itself therefore communicates the notion of the loss (or misplacement?) of presence and reminds us of recent questionings about ontological grounding, of how the text can only be about nothing, or even the absence of nothing. (It has become difficult to fix on "about" as "has as a subject"; it seems always to suggest what the writing is *doing*.) We are left with the materiality of the text. Similarly Melville's subtitle, in the end, points to the lack of meaning and clarity endemic to ethics and idea as well as to writing itself.

38

Finally, the texts are similar in being early fictional treatments of the nature of discourse and the difficulties in truth-telling, not to mention truth-living.

What is very clear is that *Lost Illusions,* surely more than any other novel of the time, insists upon itself as an object. The palpability of ink, type, and paper is felt throughout. David Séchard, initially a poet, is fathered by the illiterate typesetter in more ways than one. He eventually turns his talents from making marks on paper to making the paper itself. Lucien remains a writer, increasingly corrupted, whereas David dedicates himself to the creation of ever-finer grades of paper and drops his vocation only at the insistence of his even more practical wife. The ink on the paper becomes nearly incidental to David as he develops a pulp made of nettles and thistles, "vegetable substances which grow in marshes and infertile soil and therefore are very cheap" (*LI* 515). The serial sketches, *feuilletons,* which Lucien contributes to the periodicals are themselves leaves, *feuilles.* The paper is paramount, derives from the ground, and exploits the poet as an ingredient ("chardon" is French for "thistle"; Lucien wants to become "de Rubempré" for social reasons only). The sections of the novel progress from "The Two Poets" (Lucien and David) through "A Great Man in Embryo" (Lucien) to "An Inventor's Tribulations" (David). Lucien has been victimized by society and by the writing profession: late in the book Petit-Claud speaks of him as a "serial novel (*LI* 665). The text includes a history and descriptions of paper-making and tells us that it owes its very existence to print and paper. Inspiration itself takes on a physicality, as ignored volumes of poetry become not only "nightingales" (*LI* 201) perched in storerooms but also "muses covered with dust, spattered with mud by passing cabs" (*LI* 244). In the city Lucien is struck by "the brutally materialistic aspect that literature could assume" (*LI* 202).

In the chapter on the history of paper-making Balzac speculates that "writing and perhaps language itself passed through the same groping stages as typography and paper-making" (*LI* 109). Daniel d'Arthez, the brightest light of the Cénacle, is said to be working on a novel "solely in order to explore the resources of language" (*LI* 214). For a novelist frequently considered a realistic chronicler of society, whose novels before *The Chouans* were not signed with his own name and were frankly composed to make money, Balzac theorizes a great deal about the nature of language. Another instance of this appears in the confrontation between Blondet, an experienced hand at the journalism business, and the novice Lucien. Blondet is startled to find that Lucien has written a review in which he simply expressed "what he thought." Emile speaks for indeterminacy and argues that in writing, "telling the truth" has no sense in any case: "'Which of us could decide between Clarissa and Lovelace or between Hector and Achilles? Who was Homer's true Hero? What did Richardson really mean? Criticism must examine every work in all its various aspects. In short we are great relativists'" (*LI* 372-73). The distance between the Cénacle and the Wooden Galleries, the tawdry haunt of the publishers, may not be so very great after all. Writing itself, in both instances, exerts a controlling force. Blondet's point of view goes beyond being a journalist's rationalization for selling out to success and vested interests. Literature is paper, ink, language—all of which are definitive, palpable, and make use of authors no matter what their artistic intentions and pretensions may be.

The difficulties inherent in determining and indicating meaning are also central to *Pierre*.[2] Like Lucien Chardon, Pierre is a son, reader, and writer who suffers through many "anxieties of influence" (to borrow the phrase from Harold Bloom). Pierre finds it impossible to discover (and to tell) the truth. He tries to cut himself away from the father (and to become his own father, as "Pierre" merges with "père") and to establish his life on a new and pure moral basis, but he cannot achieve these things and finally becomes conscious that in writing, an underived, primary, unmediated vision is not possible.[3] Characters are spoken of as texts; Pierre's life ends when the book, and his book, end. *Pierre* was Melville's last novel, a dead end, for a few years; "*Pierre* is too much like the book one can imagine being produced by its hero."[4]

As Eric Sundquist has pointed out, "the doubling in *Pierre* is dizzying indeed": "Only after Pierre is introduced as an author who has written a book suspiciously like the one we have been reading are we sure that the irony will never stop, *can* never stop" (HF 180-81). Pierre's fate is caught up in a web of life, a web of words.

There are many moments when Pierre's vision is brought up short by the fact of his text and other texts. Signifiers—portraits and pyramids as well as words, in this case—carry little unambiguous signification. Images of absence and loss are pervasive.[5] It is not enough that Pierre's father is a portrait: he is three portraits, each of which communicates contradictory signals about a lost subject who may not even have been the model for the third. The huge rock that fascinates Pierre, and which carries a cryptic inscription, is in the end inscrutable, the Terror Stone. This rock, named by Pierre the "Memnon Stone," has a "forehead-like summit," and Pierre, whose name is etymologically related to "rock," "in the profound significance of that deep forest silence," wishes it to be his "Headstone." The stone does not sing as in the ancient legend: "Memnon's sculptured woes did once melodiously resound; now all is mute" (*P* 162, 164). Equally mute, in another well-known passage, is the sarcophagus at the center of the pyramid. Ahab's fear that there may be nothing beyond paste-board masks is matched here by the discovery that discovery is impossible, that there is no body in the tomb, that there is no "unlayered substance" and that all is "surface stratified on surface" (*P* 323).

Although Pierre seeks a radical originality, and "to a mind bent on producing some thoughtful thing of absolute Truth, all mere reading is apt to prove an obstacle hard to overcome" (*P* 321), he eventually realized that as "a mortal man Shakespeare had his fathers too" (*P* 164). The only underived status belongs to the God of Plinlimmon's "Chronometricals and Horologicals." God is "the only original author" (*P* 295); the Son is the Word made Flesh. Names result from an "endless descendedness" and are "more endurable than a man, or than dynasties of men" (*P* 30). Dante, Shakespeare, the Bible, and early nineteenth-century sentimental novels are assimilated into the text. Rejection of those influences calls our attention to them and becomes a proof of their presence.

Much of Pierre's anguish as a writer grows with his awareness that the deepest thought cannot be translated into words and that words themselves, apart from authorial intention, dictate thought. He feels a profound sense of loss of control. The intriguing Isabel possesses a "nameless fascination" for him (*P* 75). Novels are false because they oversimplify and attempt to systematize "eternally unsystemizable elements." Human life "partakes of the unravelable inscrutableness of God." The greatest works possible are those which "never unravel their own intricacies, and have no proper endings; but in imperfect, unanticipated, and disappointing sequels (as mutilated stumps), hurry to abrupt intermergings with the eternal tides of time and fate" (*P* 170). "All the great books in the world are but the mutilated shadowings-forth of invisible and eternally unembodied images in the soul" (*P* 322). Melville tells us that Pierre was writing two books: the private, ideal one that demanded his blood and soul, and the public, bungled one that required only ink and paper (*P* 344). In the final episode the merging of writer and novel is complete: "Nor book, nor author of the book, hath any sequel, though each hath its last lettering!—It is ambiguous still" (*P* 402).

Other aspects of the word's control are presented as well. For example, when Isabel explains her growing feelings of humanness she mentions her "speech being sometimes before the thought; so, often, my own tongue teaches me new things" (*P* 151). Pierre is conscious of the prohibitive force of openings, as his

> printed pages now dictated to the following manuscript, and said to all subsequent thoughts and inventions of Pierre— *Thus and thus; so and so; else an ill match.* Therefore, was his book already limited, bound over, and committed to imperfection, even before it had come to any confirmed form or conclusion at all." (*P* 379-80)

Readers, too, have their own ways with Pierre's texts. One of the appreciators of "The Tear" finds a special significance in the dot (tear) over an *i* in Pierre's poem, a tear paradoxically washed away by a shower. Pierre cannot control this separation between intention and interpretation and is not aware that "tear" can also signify, as it might for us, "to rip"—the rending apart of the fate of the text from the author's designs for it.

One of the most striking parallels between *Pierre* and *Lost Illusions* relates to truly remarkable episodes in the two novels. Messages, influential if imperfectly comprehended by the protagonists, come unexpectedly to Lucien and Pierre at crucial moments in their careers. As he travels to the city to make a new beginning, Pierre discovers a pamphlet in his carriage; as Lucien contemplates suicide he finds, in the tales told him by a mysterious Spanish priest, a reason to live and to go on to the city once again. The life of this cleric, the Abbé Carlos Herrera (alias Vautrin, Jacques Collin, or Cheat-Death—Balzac's frequent villain), is an enactment of the very contrasts between absolute heavenly virtue and worldly expedience mapped out in Plinlimmon's tract on "Chronometricals and Horologicals." The man of God has realized that even in the monastery "the world is often to be found in miniature" (*LI* 650). He has embraced a Machiavellian scheme and feels that "there are no longer any laws, merely conventions." Although he says he believes in God, Herrera also feels that his "Order only believes in the temporal power" (*LI* 649). (As we see truth becoming an impossible heavenly virtue, this "temporal power" comes to include language.) Lucien is a changed writer; apparently convinced by this advice to "lie in ambush in the world of Paris" (*LI* 648), Lucien allows Herrera to become his sponsor and mentor.

Pierre, on the other hand, can make little sense of his text's meaning and continues being "the Fool of Virtue." Melville's judgments excuse Pierre's inability to act on the basis of the pamphlet's theme of a virtuous expediency, as Plinlimmon's work is said to be not so much the solution to a problem as a statement of it. It is not even that: it is an excellently illustrated re-statement of a problem" (*P* 243). We are later told that Plinlimmon's pamphlet is based on notes "taken down at random, and bunglingly methodized by his young disciples" (*P* 329). Well might Pierre join his model, Hamlet, in having his resolution "sicklied o'er the pale cast of thought." Pierre's copy of Plinlimmon's essay is torn and therefore without a conclusion. It has an enigmatic heading followed by a prefatory note that it is "not so much the Portal, as part of the temporary Scaffold to the Portal of this new Philosophy" (*P* 244). The number of removes of the text—already an abandoned text—from a real source is, however, no greater than that of any philosophical text's from a vital center:

> That profound Silence, that only Voice of our God, which I before spoke of; from that divine thing without a name, those imposter philosophers pretend somehow to have got an answer; which is as absurd, as though they should say they had got water out of stone; for how can a man get a Voice out of Silence? (*P* 242)

One story Herrera tells to convince Lucien not to commit suicide is another important "inner text" and the most bizarre tale of the novel. An artisan's son—who writes and is obviously likened to Lucien—makes such an impression on his noble employer's wife that she later marries him despite a bad habit, a growing compulsion to chew paper. At first satisfied with blank paper, he soon takes to "masticating manuscripts, which he found more tasty" (*P* 637). He is rescued by the Duchess from a sentence of death incurred for having eaten the Finnish Treaty! The young clerk is dedicated to his work and thus consumes texts and is consumed by them. Lines between self and text blur as we realize that the secretary feeds on what he himself has written, which generates self and which self generates, and that Chardon too, in David Séchard's experiments, is paper. Food and fetish are involved in the creative process and we, as readers, grow uneasy as we consume this text. The paper sustains us too, in that we have thoughts for food as well as food for thought.

Pierre also is a novel about "the consumption and production of literary texts" (ET 146). The pamphlet that Pierre discovers on the stage-coach is "a thin, tattered, dried-fish-like thing; printed with blurred ink upon mean, sleazy paper" (*P* 239). When Pierre meets "this inscrutable Plotinus Plinlimmon himself" (*P* 332) he feels a renewed desire to read and digest "Chronometricals and Horologicals." The pamphlet, however, is lost. Years later the worn pages are discovered by a clothesman in the lining of Pierre's coat, where they had worked their way after falling through a hole in a pocket. Melville concludes the chapter with the thought that Pierre's subsequent career seemed to prove that he had finally understood the essay and that some men know things that they only think they do not know. The pamphlet had become part of him; he was wearing it, unknown still.

"Pierre, however vain of his fame, was not at all proud of his paper." His own pages are always blowing about. He makes "allumettes of his sonnets when published" and housemaids fuel fires with his vagabond manuscripts. Although indifferent to "the primitive vestments of his immortal productions" (*P* 299) and certain that the writer's soul labors to support his body, Pierre eventually despairs and has a foretaste of death when his abused eyes ("the only visible outward symbols of that soul") rebel and "absolutely refused to look on paper." Both he and his paper become "suspended, motionless, blank" (*P* 383). Incarnation has all along been his major desideratum. Life can be unequivocally one for him only if his ideals can be made real. Only if his words, and not just his paper, could become flesh would he be content. The arbitrary nature of writing and language itself makes it impossible for Pierre to truly enter the world. Put another way, the divisions he perceives—between body and soul, the real and the ideal, the thought and its expression—are unbridgeable chasms. Whereas he is preoccupied with pure virtue and idea, Pierre knows nothing of speculators' plans to "start a paper-mill expressly for the great author" (*P* 300).[6]

The title of *Lost Illusions* thus applies to the protagonists of both novels, who discover the impossibility of returning to a "green and golden world" (*P* 23) and of establishing their lives on the ideal bases they had early conceived of. Even more importantly, the ambiguous title and the content of both books disclose the illusory nature of writing. The novels are texts, contain texts, and treat the problem of fixing a definition for text. "The fact of vacated authority" (HF 156) is implicit in what both novels say about authority figures—figures that include other books. Yet books must always influence other books. The truly illusory text here is that invisible "one" from which both of these novels have grown, there being no conclusive proof that Melville had read Balzac. Echoing William Cullen Bryant's judgment that "the native vigor of genius" can be maintained only by studying the beauties of all classes of poetry,[7] Melville concludes that the writer can remain unique, not dominated by any one past author, only when all great works are "federated in the fancy" (*P* 322). We have modern theory along with nineteenth-century texts. These novels parallel each other in such numerous, striking ways, both superficial and deeply theoretical, that what finally strikes us is their not influencing each other or deriving from a discrete earlier source. *Lost Illusions* and *Pierre* are certainly federated in *our* fancies.

NOTES

[1]Honoré de Balzac, *Lost Illusions*. Middlesex, England: Penguin Books Ltd., 1971, (Hereafter cited in the text as *LL*). Herman Melville, *Pierre, or, the Ambiguities*. New York: The New American Library of World Literature, 1964. Hereafter cited in the text as *P*.

[2]For a treatment of *Pierre* as a book about reading and writing see Edgar A. Dryden's "The Entangled Text: Melville's *Pierre* and the Problem of Reading," *Boundary* 2, 7, No. 3 (Spring 1979), 145-73. The discussion here includes a few issues also raised by Dryden, particularly those which link *Pierre* with *Lost Illusions*.

[3]Eric J. Sundquist, *Home as Found: Authority and Genealogy in Nineteenth-Century American Literature*. Baltimore: Johns Hopkins University Press, 1979. 171. Hereafter cited in the text as *HF*.

[4]Charles Feidelson, Jr., *Symbolism and American Literature.* Chicago: University of Chicago Press, 1953. 201.

[5]Edgar A. Dryden, "The Entangled Text: Melville's *Pierre* and the Problem of Reading." *Boundary 2*, 7, No. 3 (Spring 1979), 157. Hereafter cited in the text as ET.

[6]The full implications of Pierre's situation are brought out through connections with other works by Melville. Eric Sundquist states an important idea in *Moby Dick,* the novel immediately preceding *Pierre:*

> The simultaneous *consummation* and *consumption* which governs the cannibalism of *Moby-Dick*—whether literal or figurative—are entwined in the totemic festival; and not least because, as modern anthropology has often confirmed, copulation and eating, and particularly incest and cannibalism, are so often fused as either prohibited or requisite functions in a community's ritual observances. (150)

The concept further unifies, and complicates, *Pierre*, since incest is the book's notorious theme. The sexual symbolism in "The Paradise of Bachelors and the Tartarus of Maids" is clear when the seedsman surveys the women who make the envelopes for his seed: "At rows of blank-looking counters sat rows of blank-looking girls, with blank, white folders in their blank hands, all blankly folding blank paper." (Reprinted in Chase, Richard, ed. *Herman Melville: Selected Tales and Poems.* New York: Holt, Rinehart and Winston, 1950. 220. [The tale was first published in 1855]). In Balzac's novel the paper-eater is saved and finds favor with the Duchess as a result of eating the paper itself. Thoughts, expression, are insubstantial. Only with use are the virginal sheets violated; only with violation are they useful.

[7]William Cullen Bryant, "On Originality and Imitation." Reprinted in Perkins, George, ed. *American Poetic Theory.* New York: Holt, Rinehart and Winston, 1972.

5. TEXTS ENGENDERING TEXTS: A QUÉBECOIS REWRITING OF AMERICAN NOVELS

Anne Marie Miraglia

THE CREATIVE LITERARY PROCESS is in itself often the subject of the novels of the Québecois writer Jacques Poulin. His novel *Volkswagen Blues*, published in 1984, is simultaneously the story of Jack Waterman's search for his brother Theo and that of the search and discovery of the novel's genesis.[1] Accompanied by a young Métis woman named la Grande Sauterelle, Jack Waterman's quest takes him from Gaspé, Québec, across the United States via the Oregon Trail, and south to San Francisco, California. This *spatial* journey diagonally across the United States is, however, doubled by a *textual* journey covering a number of Canadian and American literary intertexts. Jack Waterman's journey parallels the pioneer's quest for the American dream, and the novel echoes this search as it is represented in the American intertexts that compose it.

One reason for this reflexivity is that Jack Waterman is a Québecois writer in search of a subject for his next novel and his Métis companion is an insatiable reader of books. Writing and reading are interdependent acts, and as such the writer is always, a priori, a reader himself. Thus, there are two types of fictitious readers in *Volkswagen Blues;* however, what I call "fictitious reader" must not be confused with Gerald Prince's and Gérard Genette's narratological notion of "narratee." The fictitious reader is exclusively present at the utterance or diegetic level, whereas the "narratee" is a construct of the enunciation. In *Volkswagen Blues,* fictitious writer and reader cross the North American continent and in so doing evoke American intertexts pertinent to their quest. The fictitious reader facilitates the integration of intertextual phenomena, which engenders the creation of Jack Waterman's future novel. His book will be identical or similar to Jacques Poulin's *Volkswagen Blues,* and it will be a response to the reading and interpretation of the intertexts that make up the novel.

Thematization or actualization of the act of reading is often a questioning of specific intertexts. What is the character reading? Why? At what moment? What are the effects of this reading on the character and on the progress of the events? And what are the connections, if any, between these intertexts and the text? In those cases where the creative literary process is the subject of the story, it is often evident that a certain type of reading precedes and influences the creative output of the fictitious writer. His writing, then, represents the reading and rewriting of specific intertexts—their rejection or assimilation. Intertextuality is thus an autorepresentational or metafictional device which attracts attention to the reception of an intertext and the production of the text.

Reading, decoding, and interpreting a message is often thematized and actualized in *Volkswagen Blues.* Its first such manifestation is the deciphering of a postcard Jack Waterman received fifteen years earlier from his brother Theo. The card reproduces a relating of the French explorer Jacques Cartier's first voyage to America in 1534. Jacques Cartier's report of the construction of the holy cross and the establishment in North America of the shield bearing three white lilies places the novel under the signs of the spiritual and material quest representative of man's discovery and settlement of America. The postcard incites Jack Waterman to undertake the search for his brother, whom he asso-

ciates with his childhood and the French past of the American continent. Consequently, Jack Waterman's and la Grande Sauterelle's journey from Gaspé, Québec, to Saint Louis, Missouri—the gateway to the
American West—traces the first exploration of America by the French
explorers. The quest is therefore geographical, historical, and literary in
nature.

Intertextuality is a means by which the autorepresentational text
furnishes a model for its interpretation. Recognition of the intertext en-
ables one to decipher literary phenomena latent in the composition and
reception of the text. According to Michael Riffaterre, reading is done
in two ways. The first is retroactive, the second is intertextual. The first
refers to the normal reading process during which the reader makes
comparisons while recognizing repetitions, variants of an identical
structure. The intertextual reading is the perception of these comparabil-
ities, but from one text to another.[2] Intertextual reading is necessary for
decoding and fully appreciating the creation of *Volkswagen Blues*. In
fact the text explicitly advocates such a reading:

> Il ne faut pas juger les livres un par un. Je veux dire: il ne
> faut pas les voir comme des choses indépendantes. Un livre
> n'est jamais complet en lui-même; si on veut le
> comprendre, il faut le mettre en rapport avec d'autres livres,
> non seulement avec les livres du même auteur, mais aussi
> avec des livres écrits par d'autres personnes. Ce que l'on
> croit être un livre n'est la plupart du temps qu'une partie
> d'un autre livre plus vaste auquel plusieurs auteurs ont
> collaboré sans le savoir. (*VB* 169)

Jack Waterman's books are juxtaposed with that of other writers on
three separate occasions. The text thus implicitly places Jack Waterman's books (and, through him, Québecois literature) in relation to
American literature. More than forty intertexts of various disciplines
comprise *Volkswagen Blues*—songs, history books, paintings, films,
photos, and of course fiction. Whereas the other intertexts are of
French, Québecois, American, and Canadian culture, the *fictional* inter-

51

texts are American except for Stevenson's *Treasure Island.* The order of their appearance is determined by the geographical advances of the journey and are as follows: John Irving's *The Hotel New Hampshire* (title given in French translation), Jack Kerouac's *On the Road,* Saul Bellow's *The Adventures of Augie March,* and Jack London's *The Valley of the Moon.* (It is interesting to mention in passing that both Jack Kerouac and Saul Bellow are American writers of French-Canadian origin.) Like *Volkswagen Blues,* three of the above-mentioned American intertexts can be categorized within the genre of American travel novels. *The Adventures of Augie March* and *The Hotel New Hampshire* do not quite qualify as travel novels, but they do involve journeys. The insertion of the American fictional intertexts is in part due to the main character's status as a writer in search of material, his preoccupation with his brother, and his desire to read books relevant to his trip (*VB* 43). All the above-mentioned intertexts, therefore, have as a dominant theme man's search for happiness, his quest of a dream, of a myth, across an unknown frontier. In most cases it is a question of America, the land of promise, and of the realization of dreams.

It is of little wonder, then, that Jack Waterman should find the postcard of Jacques Cartier's journey in Walker Chapman's book *The Golden Dream.* It is from this book that Jack Waterman takes the story of the legend of Eldorado, which makes up chapter two of *Volkswagen Blues.* Two books by Gilbert Chinard, *L'exotisme américain dans la littérature française au XVI siècle* (1911) and *L'Amérique et le rêve exotique dans la littérature française au XVIIe et au XVIIIe siècles,* have done much to trace the power of the discovery of America on the French literary imagination of the sixteenth, seventeenth, and eighteenth centuries. *Volkswagen Blues* illustrates that this fascination with the American continent and with the American dream continues and that it focuses specifically on the United States.

In *Volkswagen Blues* the American literary intertexts most revealing of the myth of the American dream and most directly associated with the creation and interpretation of Jack Waterman's future novel are

Gregory Franzwa's tourist and historical guide *The Oregon Trail Revisited* (a "rewriting" of Parkman's *The Oregon Trail*) and Jack Kerouac's *On the Road*. Franzwa's guide traces the journey and hardships of the pioneers determined to seek happiness and fortune in the wild American West. Jack Kerouac's novel represents a modern physical appropriation of the American continent imitative of the pioneer spirit of adventure, self-confidence, hopefulness, and liberty. *Volkswagen Blues* absorbs and transforms both books; it evokes the pioneer's struggle traced in *The Oregon Trail* while conducting a modern Québecois and Métis exploration of North America's French and Indian past. *Volkswagen Blues* is the reading and rewriting of all five American intertexts. It assimilates the themes of dream, myth, self-knowledge, and happiness inherent to these intertexts.

Inspired by her reading of the Russian critic Mikhaïl Bakhtin, Julia Kristeva in 1969 draws the notion of "intertextuality" from Bakhtin's concept of dialogism and interaction: "Bakhtin a en vu l'écriture comme lecture du corpus littéraire antérieur, le texte comme absorption de et réplique à un autre texte."[3] For Bakhtin and Kristeva texts engender texts: "tout texte se construit comme mosaïque de citations, tout texte est absorption et transformation d'un autre texte"(*SR* 85). Although in *Le Texte du roman* Kristeva applies her theory of intertextuality to her analysis of "Jehan de Saintré," her research is limited to the impact of intertextuality upon the production of the literary text. She, unfortunately, is not interested in its effect upon the reader and thus upon the reception of the literary text. Michael Riffaterre's notion of intertextuality, however, relies on the role of the reader and his/her participation in the production of the literary text. He, therefore, defines intertextuality as a mode of perception that orients the text's reading and eventual interpretation:

> Il s'agit d'un phénomène qui oriente la lecture du texte, qui en gouverne éventuellement l'interprétation, et qui est le contraire de la lecture linéaire. C'est le mode de perception du texte qui gouverne la production de la signifiance, alors

que la lecture linéaire ne gouverne que la production du
sens. (*II* 6)

An intertext is defined as the set of texts discovered by the reader in his
memory at the reading of a given passage: "l'ensemble des textes que
l'on peut rapprocher de celui que l'on a sous les yeux, l'ensemble des
textes que l'on retrouve dans sa mémoire à la lecture d'un passage
donné" (*II* 4). Riffaterre recognizes that the intertext as such evokes an
indefinite corpus. He cautions, however, that the intertext is governed
by textual necessities: "quelle que soit son étendue pour un lecteur
donné, [l'intertexte] a des éléments constants entièrement réglés par des
impératifs textuels."[4]

The American intertexts assimilated in *Volkswagen Blues* are im-
manent to the text and as such constitute what Riffaterre calls
"obligatory intertextuality" (*TI* 5). Jacques Paulin's novel absorbs the
intertexts without contradicting their meaning. The text, however, re-
serves the possibility of adding yet another meaning. Thus it becomes
ambivalent, the result of the juxtaposition of two sign systems.

The American intertexts, which will be examined here, are evoked
at pertinent moments in the story and share with *Volkswagen Blues* the
idea of a spiritual and material quest pertinent to the pursuit of a dream.
In Independence, the Québecois writer and the young Métis follow the
Oregon Trail, that is, the route taken in the nineteenth century by pioneers wishing to conquer the American West and aspiring to happiness
and wealth. Gregory Franzwa's guide *The Oregon Trail Revisited* provides the protagonists and, through them, the reader with the geographical and historical information necessary for the appreciation and com-
pletion of their journey. The numerous references to this guide establish
a parallel, constant throughout the novel, between three different ex-
plorations of the American continent: the modern journey undertaken
by Jack Waterman and la Grande Sauterelle, that made by the pioneers
and adventurers of the nineteenth century, and that of Jacques Cartier
and the French explorers of the sixteenth century. In all three cases the
search for happiness was made from east to west.

A similar parallelism is also a constant in Jack London's *The Valley of the Moon*. This novel is read by a vagabond whom Jack Waterman and la Grande Sauterelle meet just before they reach Fort Hall, where the trail forks north to Oregon and south to California. The vagabond is content to spend his life hitchhiking between the two, spending spring and summer in Oregon and autumn and winter in California. In fact he seems to have realized his dream, and it is most appropriate that it be this character who reads Jack London's book.

The Valley of the Moon (1913) is the story of a young Anglo-Saxon couple who, wishing to escape the violence of industrial poverty in Oakland, California, tramp north across the country to Oregon with the hopes and dream of discovering the land where they could prosper and be happy. Like *Volkswagen Blues*, Jack London's book is nostalgic. Saxon and Billy constantly evoke the struggles and fighting spirit of their ancestors who crossed the plains, mountains, and deserts to go West to the promised land, to California, the land of milk and honey. They comment upon the deterioration of America since that time due to industrialization and urbanization and, most importantly, they come to recognize the perversion of American ideals through greed and destruction. Nonetheless, Saxon and Billy do realize their dream of finding the valley of the moon, paradise on earth, and it is in this respect that Jack London is read by the vagabond and not by Jack Waterman.

Waterman's quest is impossible to realize because his happiness depends upon the discovery of his brother and through him resuscitation of the past, the innocence and happiness of his childhood and that of mythical early French America. Allusions to events recorded in *The Oregon Trail Revisited* indicate that Jack's search for his brother Theo is a nostalgic quest for his childhood and for French America. Theo is associated with the sixteenth-century French explorer Etienne Brûlé and with a nineteenth century pioneer guide from Franzwa's book.

The Oregon Trail Revisited is one of two books discovered to be in Theo's possession at the time of his imprisonment in Toronto. The second is Jack Kerouac's *On the Road*. This American travel novel also incites the Québecois writer and the Métis to break through the walls of Québec in order to explore the American continent in an attempt to physically possess it as the French explorers Louis Jolliet, Father Jacques Marquette, and Robert Cavelier de La Salle had done before them. *On the Road* and *Volkswagen Blues* share a number of themes although their style, tone, and adventures are diametrically opposed. In fact, this dramatic difference is thematized in chapter four entitled "L'écrivain idéal." The implication is that the ideal writer is, like Kerouac, a writer of spontaneous prose. Chapter twenty-nine, entitled "Les Fantômes de San Francisco," often makes references to Kerouac and *On the Road*.

In both *Volkswagen Blues* and *On the Road* the protagonist is a writer desirous of adventures, adventures that will take the form of the novel we are reading. The voyage across the United States represents an attempt to rid themselves of a certain weariness about the sedentary, solitary life of the writer suffering from his delusions and the failure of relationships. In Jack Waterman's case it is also a question of the writer's incapacity to write another novel. Both Jack Waterman and Sal Paradise wish to identify with a more spontaneous, energetic, and passionate brother figure. This is Dean Moriarty for Sal Paradise and Theo for Jack Waterman. Theo's anti-conformity and fervent lifestyle are very much like that of Dean Moriarty. Dean and Theo are heros. They represent "a new kind of American saint,"[5] and much like the pioneers they are confident of their ability to accomplish whatever they wish.[6] Jack Waterman, a timid, weak and soft-spoken Québecois, associates this manner of thinking with that of the pioneer spirit and, in general, with that which is American. Through the memory of the brother-figure Jack Waterman and Sal Paradise rediscover the innocence, freshness, and exuberance of their youth, which in both cases is evocative of America's pioneer past. Their voyage across the United States begins in the spring, is preceded by the reading of the adventures of the pioneers, and incites the writing of their own adventures.

But the brother-figure is subject to the ravages of time. With time, Dean Moriarty, an eager reader of Marcel Proust, loses his mystery, his power of speech, and with that his power to seduce others. His followers lose confidence in him and in his lifestyle, a life of senseless emptiness (*OR* 208) at the end of which awaits death. Jack Waterman's image of his brother also disintegrates as he learns of his brother's criminal activities and when he finally discovers him in San Francisco, paralyzed and without memory. The same disillusionment accompanies his nostalgic hero, Etienne Brûlé. In Jack Kerouac's novels, as in *Volkswagen Blues*, the protagonists' personal disillusionment encompasses that of the entire American continent, and with that the deception of the American dream. But this latter absorption of *On the Road*, that is, the deterioration of the brother-figure and of the American dream, is not obvious until the final chapters of *Volkswagen Blues* after our protagonists have arrived in San Francisco.

The simple reference, however, to the title of John Irving's book *The Hotel New Hampshire* very early in the novel, when the protagonists are still in Québec City, can alert the reader to the delusive nature of a dream and the blindness entailed in its pursuit. The narrator's father, Winslow Berry is a dreamer, a man who lives in the future, who imagines he can do anything, and a man determined to realize his adolescent dream of emulating the owner of the resort hotel, the Arbuthnot-by-the-Sea. Blinded by a naïve hopefulness and confidence in his ability, he unwittingly provokes the gang-rape of his daughter Franny, the death in an airplane crash of his dear wife Mary and his youngest child, Egg; a seven-year exile in Vienna spent in a climate of sex and violence among anti-Semites, prostitutes, pornographers, and terrorist radicals; the loss of his sight; Freud's death; and eventually the suicide of his daughter Lilly. And still he dreams on. Once back in the United States, still possessed by images of the man in the white dinner jacket, Win Berry wishes to purchase and restore the Arbuthnot-by-the-Sea. Lilly, the would-be writer, sees in her father a Gatsby-figure, a man in a white dinner jacket forever in pursuit of a dream that will elude him.

F. Scott Fitzgerald's great classic, *The Great Gatsby,* is an intertext to which *The Hotel New Hampshire* often refers and to which it is obviously indebted.[12] In fact, *The Great Gatsby* seems to be the source of all the novels examined here with the exception, of course, of Jack London's book. Nick Carraway recognizes in Gatsby "a heightened sensitivity to the promises of life . . . an extraordinary gift for hope, a romantic readiness," (*GG* 2) which, as we have seen, is shared by the explorers and pioneers of America and by Irving's "Win Berry," Jack London's "Saxon," Kerouac's "Dean Moriarty," and Saul Bellow's "Augie March." Jay Gatsby's tragedy, his senseless death, his illicit rise from rags to riches in the hope of one day marrying Daisy, undermines the American dream.

This is also the case in Saul Bellow's *The Adventures of Augie March,* an intertext evoked for obvious reasons when the protagonists arrive in Chicago. The novel develops the theme of brotherhood and human relationships delineated in *On the Road* and *Volkswagen Blues.* In his novel, Jacques Poulin has Saul Bellow tell our travelers: "When you're looking for your brother, you're looking for somebody" (p.110). *Volkswagen Blues* then reproduces the following final passage of *The Adventures of Augie March,* which Jack Waterman and la Grande Sauterelle find quoted in the *Petit Robert* of proper names: "I am a sort of Columbus of those near-at-hand and believe you can come to them in this immediate *terra incognita* that spreads out in every gaze."[8] What follows, however, is the tale of the extermination of the Illinois Indians at Starved Rock.

The Adventures of Augie March, like *On the Road* and *The Hotel New Hampshire,* is also a novel about the perversion and rejection of the American dream. Augie rejects the life-style chosen for him by Grandma Lausch, by Einhorn, by Mrs. Renling, by Thea, and by his brother Simon, who like a Gatsby figure adopts the American dream at the expense of his future happiness. Constantly escaping from images of success that various people try to impose upon him, Augie March, forever loyal to himself, refuses to lead a "disappointing life," refuses to abandon his "pilgrimage" toward an independent, "worth-while fate," and wishes to return to the "axial lines of life," that is to truth, love, peace, bounty, usefulness, and harmony (*AA* 454). A person full of hope, he reads books on Utopia and helps Robey with his research on human happiness.

Volkswagen Blues, then, is the reading and rewriting of these American intertexts which exploit the ageless theme of the American dream. Yet this rewriting is specifically Québecois. Jack Waterman's search for his brother and for his French ancestors who penetrated the American continent is fundamentally the search for his own identity. And his quest for identity as a Québecois writer is dependent upon a geographical and textual exploration of the United States. The search for a brother-figure in the United States implies the exploration and discovery of this part of himself and of his past, which is American and which has long been repressed. Yet Jacques Poulin's novel seems to imply that this exploration must be done with caution. As the voyage progresses, Jack Waterman's image of his brother Theo deteriorates to that of a Judah figure, as seen in the photograph evocative of Leonardo da Vinci's "Last Supper." This figure of the traitor is doubled in Etienne Brûlé, who is said to have betrayed Québec in 1629. Through textual association, Theo is then also guilty of having betrayed Québec. His abandonment of Québec results in the loss of his memory, of his ancestral tongue, of his personal identity (*VB* 266) and in his isolation vis-à-vis his Québecois brothers. After Jack Waterman's long journey from Gaspé to California in search of his brother, Theo looks at him blankly and in English tells him, "I don't know you" (*VB* 285). Jack had hoped to be able to identify with his childhood hero and as a result rediscover the happiness and confidence of his youth. The dream fails to materialize here, and consequently *Volkswagen Blues* echos, in a different voice, its American intertexts' treatment of the American dream.

NOTES

[1]Jacques Poulin, *Volkswagen Blues* (Montréal: Québec/Amérique, 1984). Hereafter cited in the text as *VB*.

[2]Michael Riffaterre, "L'intertexte inconnu", *Literature* 41 (1981): 6.

[3]Julia Kristeva, *Sémiôtiké. Recherches pour une sémanalyse.* (Paris: Seuil, 1969): 6. Hereafter cited in the text as *SR*.

[4]Michael Riffaterre, "La trace de l'intertexte", *La Pensée* 215, (1980):5. Hereafter cited in the text as TI.

[5]Jack Kerouac, *On the Road.* (New York: New American Library, 1985): 34. Hereafter cited in the text as *OR*.

[6]See *On the Road* 37 and *Volkswagen Blues* 137.

[7]F. Scott Fitzgerald, *The Great Gatsby.* (New York: Charles Scribner's Sons, 1925): 2. Hereafter cited in the text as *GG*.

[8]Saul Bellow, *The Adventures of Augie March.* (New York: The Viking Press, 1953): 536. Hereafter cited in the text as *AA*.

6. SILONE'S "MOSES" AT THE BITTER FOUNTAIN: EXODUS AS SUBTEXT

Marisa Gatti–Taylor

IGNAZIO SILONE WROTE *Fontamara* in 1930, shortly after he abandoned his high-level posts in the Italian and International Communist parties. In this, his first novel (revised in 1949), the heart-broken exile and former political activist succeeded in articulating not only the struggle of the poor peasants of his native Abbruzzi, the *cafoni*, but by extension the plight of oppressed people everywhere. Critically acclaimed as Silone's best novel, *Fontamara* was immediately translated into numerous languages, and long before its persecuted author could receive due attention in fascist Italy its tragic story evoked compassion and admiration in many parts of the world.[1] In its simplicity, *Fontamara* has been compared to an ancient tragedy; in its portrayal of a social class in conflict it has been viewed as an epic of the proletariat. A number of critics have praised it as a piece of revolutionary literature and as a model of marxist fiction.[2]

Prior scholarship, however, has neglected an important aspect of the intertextual resonances in *Fontamara*. In my paper, I argue how the novel derives its powerful impact in part from imagery, situations, and characters which echo Biblical, hence ancient and widely known, realities. Silone himself told me that the *cafoni* comprehend the Old Testament much better than the New Testament.[3] I apply this insight to *Fontamara* and analyze a series of striking parallels between the exploitation of the Israelites in Egypt and the sufferings of the *cafoni.*

The name "Fontamara" (Bitter Fountain) given by Silone to the small, impoverished village in the Abbruzzi, in which the story unfolds, strikingly recalls the Old Testament episode described in Exodus 15:23, where it is written, "They reached Marah but the water there was so bitter they could not drink it; this is why the place was named Marah."[4] Water, or the lack of it, as we shall later see, assumes a pivotal role in the struggle for survival of the Fontamaresi as it does all through the book of Exodus.

The *cafoni* are a community of landless tillers of the soil reduced to hiring themselves out as day laborers. Their moving story is told in retrospect by three of their number who have escaped a brutal fascist reprisal on the village. Having made their way to Switzerland, the fugitives locate an exiled compatriot who listens compassionately to their accounts. In the course of one night, the escaped father, mother, and son report the events that provoked their flight. Thus, Silone provides three alternating voices to describe the action which the principal narrator, a more educated individual than they, purports to record faithfully.

In the Foreword, an integral part of the novel, the author devotes considerable effort to describing the toilsome existence of the peasants. Their poverty-stricken life is rendered intolerable by the burdens laid upon them by various authorities—the Prince of Torlogna, the Piedmontese, the Fascists. Each of these governments oppresses the *cafoni* with taxes, hard labor, and all manner of abuse. While most of the *cafoni* work as farmhands and daylaborers, many also work at making bricks in a factory belonging to a Pharaoh figure, a powerful unnamed businessman referred to as the "Impresario" (*F* 52) (translated as "Contractor"). In the Book of Exodus we read that the Egyptians made the Israelites' "lives unbearable with hard labor, work with clay and with brick, all kinds of work in the fields; they forced on them every kind of labor" (Ex. 1:15). Early in the narration, therefore, there emerges a vague parallel between the Italian civic leaders and the Egyptians, and between the *cafoni* and the Israelite slaves, prototypes of an oppressed people.

There is another basis on which the parallel between the *cafoni* and the Israelites stands, and that is the pastoral imagery in the novel. Although the Fontamaresi are not shepherds, the narrator sometimes describes them not only as shepherds but as sheep. In the Foreword, the village itself is depicted as a flock of dark sheep with the church bell-tower as its shepherd (*F* 10). Likewise, after the *cafoni* are taken by truck to Avezzano, where they are forced to cheer the authorities under false pretenses and are subsequently ridiculed and abused, the *cafone*/narrator states that the men stood like a flock of sheep without a sheep dog (*F* 123). Indeed, the *cafoni* see themselves as sheep without a shepherd, aware of how they have been betrayed by their lawyer, Don Circostanza, and their priest, Don Abbacchio, the traditional claimants to the role of shepherds. Martin McLaughlin aptly points out that the implicit question throughout the novel is, Who is the true shepherd of the black sheep of Fontamara?[5] Silone confirms Berardo Viola's emerging leadership role with a simile of him as shepherd, when he and the other *cafoni* return to Fontamara after the fascists have ravaged it and raped many of the women. We are told that he takes the woman he loves in his arms with the easy gesture of a shepherd carrying a lamb (*F* 147). This image and several allusions to the suffering Christ, together with Berardo's martyrdom, have led many critics to view Berardo as a Christ figure. By suggesting Exodus as subtext, I propose to reveal a new facet of Bernardo's persona based on Mosaic similarities.

This tacit analogy between the *cafoni* and the Hebrews pierces to the surface in an off-hand remark made by the *cafone*/narrator to a well-dressed stranger trying to gather signatures on an unidentified document. The wary peasant demands to know which tax is being introduced, but the dumbfounded bureaucrat provides no response. `The *cafone* adds, "Quello mi guardò come se avessi parlato ebraico" (*F* 27)

(He looked at me as if I had been talking Hebrew) (25) One wonders whether the English translations deliberately retain the language as "Hebrew" rather than substituting the word "Greek," which in my opinion would be a more idiomatic translation. In any case, the Italian cliché used to signify unintelligible speech acquires metaphoric import in our study of the affinities between the two suffering peoples.

Like the Hebrews in Egyptian bondage, Silone's *cafoni* are defenseless, yet they pose a threat to the authorities. They see themselves as provoking fear and wrath among the ruling powers simply by their increasing numbers, as is told of the Hebrews in Exodus 1:12: "But the more they were crushed, the more they increased and spread, and men came to dread the sons of Israel." For this reason, Zompa explains to Berardo, wars and epidemics are

> invenzioni dei Governi per diminuire il numero dei cafoni. Si vede che adesso siamo di nuova troppi" (*F* 101)

> government devices to reduce the number of *cafoni*. It's obvious there are too many of us again. (75)

Later, when the *cafoni* are attacked by *carabinieri* at the official partition of the irrigation spring, Zompa again states that war has been declared on the *cafoni*: "Siamo in troppi" (*F* 168) (There are too many of us) (120). The *carabinieri* in fact view the peasants as people destined to suffer, much like the Egyptian overseers regarded the Hebrews. Thus, the *cafoni* too are a "chosen people" of sorts: they are called to a life of suffering. However, for them there is no manna, no quail, no pillar of fire and smoke for protection. Nevertheless, they also view themselves as Old Testament people.

> Per chi non ha pane bianco, per chi ha sola pane di granoturco, è come se Cristo non fosse mai stato. Come se la redenzione non fosse mai avvenuta. Come se Cristo dovessa ancora venire (*F* 162)

For those who have no white bread, who have only dark bread, it is as if Christ had never been, as if the Redemption had never taken place, as if Christ were still to come). (116)

To the women who have come to town to protest on behalf of Fontamara when it was rumored that the water supply would be rerouted, the *carabinieri* respond disdainfully that these women are "carne abituata a soffrire" (*F* 48) (flesh used to suffering) (40).

The greatest causes of the *cafoni's* misery are lack of water and lack of land. Theirs is a continual desert experience, since God Himself often withholds rain and turns their already infertile countryside into drought-stricken land (*F* 176). Like the Jews in the time of Moses, they live with the frustrated hope of possessing the Promised Land, in their case the fertile plains of Fucino. These are the basic similarities between Exodus and *Fontamara*, similarities that could no doubt pertain to other works about the poor throughout the world. But what I have found remarkable in my study of Exodus as subtext of *Fontamara* is the number of Old Testament echoes that appear at times like transformations, mirror-images, and even distortions of Biblical episodes throughout Silone's book. These allusions could have come to Silone quite naturally as a result of his never having known in his childhood any literature except the Bible.[6]

Let us take, for example, the plagues visited upon Egypt described in Exodus, chapters 6 through 11. Berardo Viola, who like Moses becomes a reluctant leader among the *cafoni*, makes a series of threats reminiscent of the plagues against the Contractor/Pharaoh, an unnamed developer who has taken possession of the land and is about to monopolize Fontamara's water supply as well (*F* 88). In pronouncing the threats, Berardo sounds even more like Yahweh rather than Moses. He advises the *cafoni* as follows:

> Mettetegli fuoco alla conceria e vi restituirà l'acqua senza discutere. E se non capisce l'argomento, mettetegli fuoco al deposito dei legnami. E se non gli basta, con una mina fategli saltare la fornace dei mattoni. E se è un idiota e con-

tinua a non capire, bruciategli la villa di notte, quando è a letto con donna Rosalia. Solo così riavrete l'acqua. Se non lo fate, verrà il giorno che l'Impresario vi prenderà le figlie e le venderà al mercato. (*F* 88)

Set fire to his tannery, and he'll give you back your water without arguing. If he doesn't understand, set fire to his timberyard. And if that isn't sufficient, blow up his brickworks. And if he's a fool and still doesn't understand, burn down his villa at night while he's in bed with Donna Rosalia. That's the only way to get back your water. If you don't do as I say, the day will come when he'll take your daughters and sell them in the marketplace. (66)

Later at the fateful dividing of the water supply, it is the women who cry out:

> *le maledizioni più terribili che venissero loro in mente, con i pugni rivolti contro il cielo.*
> *'Possano perdere tanto sangue, per quanta acqua vogliono rubarci.'*
> *Possano piangere tante lagrime per quanta acqua vogliono rubarci.'*
> *'Che i rospi nascano nel loro stomaco.'*
> *'Che le serpi acquatiche nascano nel loro stomaco.'*
> *'Che nessuno di essi possa rivedere la moglie e i figli.'*
> *. . . 'Possano morire nel deserto.'*
> *'Possano finire nel fuoco eterno'* (*F* 172)

The most dreadful curses they could think of.
'May they lose as much blood as the water they are robbing us of.'
'May they weep as many tears as the water they are robbing us of.'
'May toads be born in their bellies.'
'May sea serpents be born in their bellies.'
'May none of them ever see their wives and children again.'

. . . 'May they die in the wilderness.'
'May they end up in everlasting fire.' (123).

Earlier in the novel, the women's march through the sun-baked countryside into town in the dusty, noontime heat stands out as a cruel parody of the Jews' wandering in the desert, since the women's efforts lead nowhere. As the author states in his Foreword, "L'oscura vicenda dei Fontamaresi è una monotona via crucis di confoni affamati di terra" (*F* 14) (The obscure history of Fontamara is that of a monotonous calvary of land-hungry *cafoni)* (17).[7]

The most curious and perhaps grotesque transposition of an important Exodus event, however, is the parting of Fontamara's water supply. In this incident, the authorities allocate three-fourths of the water to the Contractor/Pharaoh and the "remaining" three-fourths to the *cafoni,* while the latter look on in consternation (*F* 169). This anti-miracle takes place without Berardo/Moses' intervention, or perhaps in spite of it. His absence, in fact, causes suspicion and fear among the *cafoni,* who view him as their leader and their only hope of rebellion (*F* 180).

As in the case of Moses, Berardo Viola is a pivotal figure who merits close study. Although most critics agree that the true protagonist of the novel is the town of Fontamara and its people collectively, Berardo is the one *cafone* who singles himself out by word and deed.[8] A physically powerful young man of independent ideas and irascible temperament—he first appears in the narration smashing the village street lamps, since no electricity has been available for months (*F* 35)— Berardo devotes much of his time to secretly avenging fellow *cafoni* who have been wronged by the authorities. "Egli non lasciava impunita nessuna ingiustizia che ci venisse dal capoluogo" (*F* 86) (He left unrequited no wrong that came to us from the local town) (65). In that he recalls Moses, who impulsively slew an Egyptian for beating a fellow Hebrew (Ex. 2:11). Berardo too is betrayed by one of his own to the authorities, but, like Moses, instead of punishing the informant he decides to go into hiding for a time (*F* 80). Berardo's mother foretells his end when she says, "Se deve morire impiccato, non sarà certo per il denaro, ma per l'amicizia" (F, 86) (if he's really going to die on the gallows, it won't be because of money but because of friendship) (65).

Berardo's single passion is the hope of farming his own land. It consumes him. He speaks of little else: "'La terra del Fucino,' ripeteva 'quella è la terra benedetta'" (F 111) ("The Fucino land is the promised land," he kept saying) (82). In an effort to till his own field and in his eyes to become worthy of Elvira, the saintly girl he loves, he works day and night to cultivate the mountainous terrain given to him in a swindle by the wily lawyer, Don Circostanza. After months of backbreaking work, Berardo boasts of having conquered the mountain. But his triumph ends suddenly when, after three days of soft rain and thick black clouds encircling the mountaintop, his field of corn seedlings collapses down the slope, leaving an enormous ditch in its place (F 85). I find in Berardo's travail on the mountaintop and his eventual crushing disappointment a faint echo of Moses' labors on Mount Sinai and his distress upon his decent (Ex 32:19–21).[9]

Unlike Moses, however, Berardo rejects the intervention of God in the peasants' daily struggles (F 146). Only grudgingly does he allow the devil an occasional escapade, whereas for the other *cafoni* God, Christ, and the Law of Moses are frequently, although not always reverently, invoked.[10] As for the devil, they are sure that the evil one himself has taken over their land and their water and is present in their midst in the person of the Contractor.[11] Even their decadent priest views that mysterious individual as the devil personified and confesses to the Church's helplessness in dealing with Satan (F 78). Nevertheless, the narrator has placed Berardo between two Madonna-like women: Maria Rosa, his mother, and Elvira, the one he loves.[12] His feelings toward Elvira remain unexpressed until the tragic fascist attack on Fontamara, when, after taking the unconscious Elvira to her home, Berardo sleeps with her (F 147). This act, never described by the narrator and brought to light gradually and indirectly in the *cafone*/narrator's account, is all but ignored by critics.[13] Yet, I suggest that it determines to a great extent both persons' ultimate acts of self-sacrifice.

In Berardo's case, the conjugal act at first removes his freedom to risk, to dare, to lead others to rebellion while it intensifies his commitment to do all within his power to acquire a plot of arable land and become the head of his family. This drastic change in Berardo saddens Elvira, who reminds him that she fell in love with him because he was different from the others.(*F* 187). In spite of her strong statement, Berardo leaves for Rome in a fruitless search for work. After many misadventures, his resources exhausted, he receives word that Elvira is dead. He is imprisoned shortly afterward because he happens to be in a place where a packet of revolutionary leaflets is found. A young student from Avezzano is arrested at the same time. While in their cell, Berardo and the Avezzanese discuss the activities of the "Solito Sconosciuto" (the Mystery Man), the agitator who is responsible for the leaflets. This anonymous prophet-figure is the object of the *carabinieri's* intense search, and his clandestine actions arouse Berardo's sense of a calling. Having lost Elvira, the one person for whom he was willing to live, Berardo is once again free to risk everything.

During Berardo's absence, Elvira undertakes a pilgrimage to the sanctuary of the Madonna della Libera with Maria Grazia, one of the women who had been raped during the fascists' raid on Fontamara. At the altar of the Virgin, Elvira asks the Madonna to intercede for Berardo's salvation. In exchange for the grace, Elvira offers up her own life. No sooner has she uttered her prayer than her whole body begins to burn with an intense fever. She becomes, in a way, Berardo's burning bush: "cominciò a bruciare come una fascina di rami secchi cui fosse stato improvvisamente appiccato il fuoco" (*F* 226) (she had begun to burn like a bundle of dry sticks to which a match has been put) (160).[14] Elvira's sacrificial act of faith, of which Berardo remains ignorant, loosens the bond which had begun to enslave him into admiring the Contractor and even approving of his acts (*F* 198). He had set out for Rome determined to do everything in his power to succeed in his goal to own land. In Rome, he discovered the god of this world, Money, and his place of worship, Banks.

La nostra rovina ... forse è stata di aver continuato a
credere al vecchio dio, mentre sulla terra adesso ne regna
uno nuovo (*F* 195)

Perhaps our ruin ... was to have gone on believing in the
old God while a new one now reigns over the world. (140)

Through Elvira's atoning death, Berardo breaks free of the power of
Mammon. He not only finds his old self but he transcends it by deliberately identifying himself as the Mystery Man. After reading the leaflet
which describes Fontamara's plight, Berardo resolves to die so that its
message might be spread (*F* 222). Thanks to his sacrificial act, the real
revolutionary agent can continue his efforts to publish the truth about
Fontamara and its *cafoni*. Thus, the shepherd Berardo assumes the identity of a prophet and the controversial pamphlet becomes a secular echo
of Moses' decalogue. It provides a redemptive perspective in the face of
tragedy.

The change that this paper brings about among the *cafoni* is proof
of its redemptive power. Early in the novel, the reader is made aware of
the bitter struggles among the *cafoni*. Even in the Foreword, the narrator refuses to idealize them. They can be petty, cruel, even vicious toward each other. The *cafone*/narrator confesses that even between himself and his brother-in-law, when it was a question of claiming land or
water, "nessuno di noi era disposto a sacrificarsi per l'altro" (*F* 79)
(neither of us was willing to sacrifice himself for the other) (60). But
Berardo accepts to die for another individual, one he does not even
know. He is conscious of the originality of his choice: "Sarò il primo
cafone che non muore per sè, ma per gli altri" (*F* 222) (It will be the
first time that a *cafone* dies, not for himself, but for others) (157).
Conversely, if he betrays the real prophet, he realizes that centuries will
pass with no change in Fontamara's conditions.

At the end Berardo, like Moses, does not enter into the Promised
Land. Rather, he leaves behind the greatest of struggles, the *cafoni's*
Jericho. Scarpone, the man who, according to the narrator, inherited

Berardo's ways, assumes the "Joshua" role by leading the peasants' efforts to write, publish, and distribute their own stenciled paper entitled "Che fare?" (*F* 228) (What Are We To Do?) (162). This daring document provokes the fascist reprisal which destroys the town and necessitates the three refugee/narrators' flight to Switzerland. Thus, the tragic conclusion is also a hopeful beginning, since Fontamara's story will indeed be heard, again and again. It is a passover in its own right.

Our study of the parallels between Silone's book and Exodus has brought to light a number of dynamic points of reference centered around imagery, situations, and characters, all of which generate a larger context for the modern Italian novel. The principal points were the Contractor/Pharaoh and his *cafoni*/slaves, echoes of the plagues of Egypt, the figure of the reluctant hero as shepherd and prophet, the parting of the water, the desert and mountaintop experiences, the life-changing document, and even the burning bush. In searching them out; it was not my intention to prove that Silone had the Bible in mind when writing or revising his novel. It is my hope, however, that by highlighting the intertextual import of Exodus in *Fontamara*, my essay will enhance the reader's understanding of one of the novel's deeply-rooted sources of pathos.

NOTES

[1]Carmelo Aliberti, *Come Leggere 'Fontamara' di Ignazio Silone* (Milano: Mursia, 1977), pp. 48-51. The most extensive presentation in a single volume of Silone's works and their critical responses remains Luce D'Eramo's *L'Opera di Ignazio Silone, Saggio critico e guida bibligrafica* (Milano: Mondadori, 1971). Both versions of *Fontamara* are dealt with on pages 30 to 76. These include an overview of critical writers. I should like to thank Professor D'Eramo for including my Master of Arts essay on Bernanos and Silone on page 498 of her vol-

ume and also correct a very minor point. She incorrectly identifies my essay as having been presented at the University of Detroit, whereas it was done at Wayne State University.

[2]In September, 1969, I was granted several interviews with Ignazio Silone at his residence in Rome. Since he had been awarded the Prix Jérusalem in March, 1969, we talked, among other things, about Judaism and related subjects. One of his remarks was to the effect that the peasants of his area knew and understood the Old Testament better than the New Testament. This statement led me to search for indications of this observation in his writings about them. More recently, I have corresponded with the author's widow, Darina Silone, on the topic of Biblical aspects of Silone's writings. In her gracious and lengthy response, dated October 10, 1985, she writes: "I think your project of research on 'gli aspetti biblici di Silone' is serious, original, excellent. (...) of course I know that Silone's Christian roots were very deep and to my knowledge have never received any serious scholarly treatment."

[3]The Bible verses are from *The Jerusalem Bible*, Reader's Edition, ed. Alexander Jones (Garden City, New York: Doubleday & Company, Inc 1966). Silone wrote in his essay entitled "Martin Buber," *Tempo Presente*, X (July 1965), 6, that the Jerusalem edition of the Bible was his favorite. His widow, Darina Silone, also points out that *La Sainte Bible*, translated into French under the direction of the Biblical School of Jerusalem (Paris: Les Editions du Cerf, 1956), was Silone's favorite version, along with Martin Buber's translation of the Old Testament, see "Premessa," *Serverina* (Milano: Mondadori, 1981), 20.

[4]The edition of *Fontamara* which I cite throughout the text of my essay within parentheses was published in Milano by Mondadori in 1966. The English translations are taken from *Fontamara*, trans. by Eric Mosbacher, with an Introduction by Irving Howe (New York: New American Library, Meridian Classic, 1981). For this source, only the page numbers are indicated within parentheses.

[5]Martin McLaughlin, "Imagery in the Two Versions of Silone's *Fontamara*," *Association of Teachers of Italian Journal* (Summer 1986), 47, pp. 37–38.

[6]Edmond Wilson, "Two Survivors: Malraux and Silone," *New Yorker*, 21 (8 September, 1945), 85. On Silone's Christian roots, see also Piero Aragno, *Il Romanzo di Silone* (Ravenna: Longo, 1975), pp. 156–158.

[7]One of Silone's main themes in *Fontamara* is the need for individual, private ownership of land by those who work it. I find it curious, therefore, that the novel is nevertheless considered by some critics as an exemplary piece of socialist marxist literature.

[8]Argno, 32.

[9]Here, Berardo can also be seen as a Christ figure (*F* 85). It should be noted that the references to Christ usually relate to the events of Passover week, and more specifically, to Good Friday.

[10]*Fontamara*, pp. 31, 32, 34, 38, 39, 47, 57, 60, 68, 71, 102, 156.

[11]*Fontamara*, pp. 58–62, 69, 77.

[12]Maria Rosa clearly embodies the Sorrowful Mother (*F* 86), while Elvira recalls the young Virgin. She is referred to as a "madonnina" (*F* 92), and is even mistaken for an apparition of the Virgin Mary (*F* pp. 145-146).

[13]In an essay entitled "Il Mestiere di scrivere," in *Tempo Presente*, VII (August 1962), 563, Silone describes his aversion to the abundance of gratuitous eroticism in contemporary writings, while at the same time refusing to apply censorship or other bureaucratic expedients to avoid it.

[14]Silone includes a similar though less tragic episode in his novel *Il Seme sotto la neve* (Milano: Mondadori, 1950), 430. The heroine Faustina suffers from sudden, unbearable headaches which she traces to a lengthy prayer made during a retreat when she was a young girl. In it, she had asked Jesus to let her wear his crown of thorns from time to time, and as with Elvira, her request was granted.

7. POETRY AND LANGUAGE: INTERTEXTUALITY IN THE WORKS OF JOSÉ ANGEL VALENTE

Anita M. Hart

INTERTEXTUALITY, according to Barbara Johnson in *A World of Difference,* "designates the multitude of ways a text has of not being self-contained, of being traversed by otherness" (116). On the subject of poetry, Johnson writes of a vitality generated by intertextuality:

> One might say . . . that for modern theorists of intertextuality, the language of poetry is structured like an unconscious. The integrity and intentional self-identity of the individual text are put into question in ways that have nothing to do with the concepts of originality and derivativeness, since the very notion of a self-contained literary 'property' is shown to be an illusion. When read in its dynamic intertextuality, the text becomes differently energized, traversed by forces and desires that are invisible or unreadable to those who see it as an independent, homogeneous message unit, a totalizable collection of signifieds" (116-17).

Textual interrelationships in the works of José Angel Valente reveal his originality and the dynamic quality of being "traversed by otherness."

75

A major figure in the post-Spanish Civil War literary world, Valente is a well-known poet and critic of poetry and prose. Over a period of thirty years, beginning with *A modo de esperanza* in 1955, he has published seventeen individual collections of poetry, several anthologies, and significant works of criticism. Among his collections are *Poemas a Lázaro* (1960, *La memoria y los signos* (1966, *Breve son* (1968), *El inocente* (1970), and the anthology *Punto cero (Poesía 1953-1979)* (1980). Valente's most recent collections include *Tres lecciones de tinieblas* (1980), *Mandorla* (1982), and *El fulgor* (1984). His reputation is also based on such critical works as *Las palabras de la tribu* (1971) and *La piedra y el centro* (1982).[1]

One theme that provides a unifying thread for Valente's prolific and multifaceted production is that of the poet's own investigation into the purpose, nature, and art of poetic creation. References within his texts to poetry, writing, and language and the use of the term "word" in Valente's poetry and prose are frequently associated with the works of poets and writers whose production Valente has examined. This study investigates the intertextual elements that reveal connections between Valente's ideas and those of a diversity of literary figures, including T. S. Eliot, San Juan de la Cruz, María Zambrano, Stéphane Mallarmé, José Lezama Lima, Friedrich Hölderlin, Mircea Eliade, and Octavio Paz. Textual echoes from these writers' works and from the Bible, as observed in Valente's poetry and prose, emphasize Valente's focus on the concepts of poetry and linguistic expression.[2]

The intertextual elements that I have chosen to examine revolve around the subjects of poetry, the poet, and the poetic word, as these are linked to Valente's search for poetic expression, for understanding of man's existence, and for an approach to an original creative principle or the sacred. Valente states in his often-cited essay "Conocimiento y communicación" that poetry is a means to knowledge: "la poesía es, antes de cualquier otra cosa, un medio de conocimiento de la realidad" (*Las palabras de la tribu* 4). The poet pursues a method of discovery in which the process of creating the poem, initially "un sondeo en lo oscuro," produces a new awareness (6). Valente also stresses the role of poetry in restoring to language an essential quality or truth, not present in what he calls instrumental language. In the progression of his views on poetry, as observed in an examination of Valente's critical works, he describes the poetic experience as a vision and revelation of essential principles or truths that are usually concealed or unexpressable. Poetic creation provides an avenue toward enlightenment as it offers an expansion of the limits of man's understanding and his capacity for linguistic expression. As Valente states in his recent *La piedra y el centro*, a collection of essays in which he studies mysticism and includes observations on poetic theory, the word of the mystic and the word of the poet are concerned with the limits of experience and understanding, the limits of language, and thus with the extension of these limits (76). For Valente, the poet is a searcher and an illuminator, and the poetic word permits manifestation or revelation of truth.

A line from the poetry of Stéphane Mallarmé emphasizes Valente's idea that poetry has the potential to restore the expressive capacities of language. In José Batlló's *Antología de la nueva poesía española* Valente was asked to comment on what the function of poetry in Spain should be. Valente responded that poetry has to re-establish validity lost in public or false language and that when it does this, poetry restores truth to language (340). For Valente, this is a radically social function of art and another form of giving a purer meaning to the words of the tribe. Valente echoes Mallarmé's words "Donner un sens plus pur aux mots de la tribu," from "Le Tombeau d'Edgar Poe" (Bosley 174), when he states that one aspect of the role of poetry is "dar un sentido más puro a las palabras de la tribu" (340). Mallarmé's words also appear in the title of Valente's collection of critical essays, *Las palabras de la tribu*.

In Batlló's anthology, when asked to define his poetry and the direction of its evolution, Valente offered a poem as his answer. That

INTERTEXTUALITY IN LITERATURE AND FILM

poem is "Forma," which appears in *Breve son*. In this selection textual elements from the works of T. S. Eliot and the Spanish philosopher María Zambrano emphasize Valente's concept of poetry as enlightenment and the role of poetry in restoring validity and truth to language.

> *El residuo que sólo nos deja*
> *lo que ha sido llama.*
> *La materia del sueño y del tiempo*
> *en la ardiente raíz de la dura palabra,*
> *hecha piedra en su luz*
> *como queda la rosa quemada.[3]*

The terms dealing with the primal element of fire indicate Valente's concept of poetry as illumination and the necessity of purgation as a step toward recovering quality and vitality in language. The words "llama," "ardiente," and "luz" refer to the illumination and inspiration involved in the creation of poetry, to the enlightenment and knowledge that poetry offers, and to purification and regeneration. According to J. E. Cirlot's *A Dictionary of Symbols*, fire is associated with life, health, and spiritual energy. It is a mediator between forms that vanish and forms in creation . . . a symbol of transformation and regeneration" (105). The flame, for Cirlot, "symbolizes transcendance" (108), and light is associated with spirit, morality, intellect, and creative force (187-88).

Valente's "Forma" is the concretization of the creative energy or impulse: the illuminative, transcendental flame is reduced to solid form, and the material of dream and of time is converted to stone or rock. These transformations are indications of a change of state from a dynamic force to a static, concrete form. T. S. Eliot in "Burnt Norton" accentuates the "form" as the means to static perfection and a state of unity:

> . . . Only by the form, the pattern
> Can words or music reach

> The stillness, as a Chinese jar still
> Moves perpetually in its stillness. (121)

In Valente's poem, form is associated with the stillness and solidity of the stone. In his recent *La piedra y el centro*, Valente states that stone is a symbol of the center and of totality (12). The visible, concrete form or "piedra" represents the poet's attempt to capture an illuminative essence. In this poem Valente seems to be suggesting the limitations inherent in his own effort to capture in words or to reduce to form an insight or a vision associated with the symbolic flame or dream. For both Eliot and Valente, form permits the manifestation of an essential, vital totality or unity, the stillness and the stone.

> All manner of things shall be well
> When the tongues of flame are in-folded
> Into the crowned knot of fire
> And the fire and the rose are one. (145)

The final line stresses the combination of fire, symbolizing purgation and purification, and the rose, suggesting perfection, unity, beauty, love, and harmony.

The subject of regenerating language is also evident in Eliot's "Little Gidding," which contains a reference to Mallarmé's phrase "To give a purer meaning to the words of the tribe":

> Since our concern was speech, and speech impelled us
> To purify the dialect of the tribe
> And urge the mind to aftersight and foresight. (141)

The concept of purgation preceding regeneration and unity is evident in Valente's image of the burned rose and in the phrase "la ardiente raíz de la dura palabra," which suggests an enlightening, burning verbal expression. One aspect of Valente's poetic creation is a critical, occasionally harsh and sarcastic approach, intended to bring about recovery of

79

quality in language and poetry, as well as in aspects of man's society. Valente's own poetry, particularly after the collection *Breve son* (1968), which contains "Forma," and through the early 1970's, includes selections that emphasize destruction and purgation as preliminary steps to regeneration of the essential, vital capacity of language. As Valente has stated in his essay "Ideología y lenguaje," "sólo la palabra poética, que por el hecho de ser creadora lleva en su raíz la denuncia, restituye al lenguaje su verdad" (*Las palabras de la tribu* 253).[4] For Eliot, it is the Word, symbolizing God, which is eternal, existing at the beginning and at the end, capable of restoring totality and unity to man's existence.[5]

The words "sueño," "llama," "palabra," and "luz" in Valente's poem "Forma" call to mind significant concepts in the works of Spanish philosopher María Zambrano. Valente, in *Las palabras de la tribu*, studies Zambrano's *El sueño creador*, where the philosopher focuses on the dream of the person that leads to an awakening of the deepest, most authentic part of the self. This awakening, for Zambrano, is a creative, poetic action (39). In *Claros del bosque*, Zambrano associates the term "flame" with vision, freedom and beauty; and she acknowledges the purifying, energizing, illuminating characteristics of the flame (5). Zambrano's discussions of dreams, awakening, enlightenment, and creativity lead directly to the concept of the word as a creative force. Both Zambrano and Valente focus on the poetic word and its ability to reveal truth and to liberate language from limitations and overuse.

Valente's poem "Palabra," from the collection *Material memoria*, is dedicated to María Zambrano. This cryptic poem suggests that the word offers a state of freedom and potential illumination. Although there is a sense of incompleteness because of the disassociation of elements from factors that are usually related, there is a clear indication of unlimited possibility of verbal expression.

> Palabra
> hecha de nada.
> Rama

en el aire vacío.
Ala
sin pájaro.
Vuelo
sin ala.
órbita
de qué centro desnudo
de toda imagen.
Luz,
donde aún no forma
su innumerable rostro lo visible. (*Punto cero* 464)

In *El sueño creador*, Zambrano studies "La palabra," stating the association of the word with freedom and the capacity of the word to create the true present reality and truth. The philosopher writes: "La palabra, ella misma, de por sí, es libertad" (44). She explains the capacity of the word to create the true present in the sense that through the word time ceases to be potential and movement and becomes actualized and concrete. Zambrano concludes: "Se trata, entonces, de la verdad" (45), indicating the link between the word and the establishment of truth and reality.

In Valente's poem "Palabra" the word consists of nothing. This undefined, unidentified word is free of predetermined meanings and relationships. This is the word that Zambrano equates with freedom. In Valente's poem, elements existing independently of phenomena with which they are usually linked indicate freedom from normal conditions and an expansion of possibilities. The branch (line 3), unconnected to a tree, exists alone in the empty air. The wing (line 5) is not a part of a bird. Flight (line 7) occurs, paradoxically, without a wing. The role of the word in offering freedom and potential to language is evident in the concept of a zero point, as stated in the preface to Valente's anthology *Punto cero:* "La palabra ha de llevar el lenguaje al punto cero, al punto de la indeterminación infinita, de la infinita libertad" (7). The final six lines of the poem "Palabra" emphasize the free and as yet undetermined nature of what is to be revealed. The nouns "órbita" and Luz," positioned similarly on the printed page and standing alone, are followed by modifiers that indicate both incompleteness and potential fulfillment. The orbit (line 9) actually has nothing around which it circles. The term "centro desnudo" (line 10) signals an emptiness and an openness. The "luz" is modified by a clause indicating that nothing visible has yet appeared in that light. The image "su innumerable rostro" suggests an as yet unidentified, unlimited manifestation of reality through the illuminative poetic word, language freed from predetermined conditions and capable of revealing truth. As Zambrano has stated, "La palabra, ella misma, de por sí es libertad" (*El sueño creador* 44).

The term "lo visible" in the last line of the poem "Palabra" is associated with a statement by the Cuban writer José Lezama Lima: "La luz es el primer animal visible de lo invisible." The sentence appears as the epigraph to Valente's collection *Material memoria* (*Punto cero* 459), which contains "Palabra." The invisible, that which the freedom of the poetic word is to reveal or to let manifest, is the subject that Valente, Zambrano, and Lezama Lima are concerned with.

The role of poetry in revealing an invisible essence or truth and the poet's attempt to express the ineffable represent a significant aspect of Valente's concept of poetry. It is on this subject and the related topic of an approach to a universal creative principle, such as the *logos*, that I observe textual interrelationships between Valente's writing and that of San Juan de la Cruz, José Lezama Lima, Octavio Paz, Mircea Eliade, and Friedrich Hölderlin.

In the essay "La hermenéutica y la cortedad del decir" Valente acknowledges the limitations of language, the material with which the poet works. This insufficiency of language is the "corto decir," a term that Valente cites from Dante's *Paradiso* (*Las palabras de la tribu* 63-64). Language is "the voice of a silence" (64) in that language is the poet's medium for attempted expression of the profound, the ineffable, "lo indecible." This silence that offers potential for expression is an absolute or a totality of meaning. According to Valente, it is the tendency of the inexpressable to seek expression: "Paradójicamente, lo indecible busca el decir . . ." (66).

Words and concepts from the works of San Juan de la Cruz appear frequently in Valente's essays and in his poetry. Both the mystic and the poet deal with the subject of the potential of language to express the ineffable and the poet's attempt to put into words an experience that defies articulation. In the prologue to *Subida del Monte Carmelo*, cited by Valente in the essay "La hermenéutica y la cortedad del decir," San Juan de la Cruz writes of the difficulty of saying or expressing the union of the soul with the divine:

> . . . porque son tantas y tan profundas las tinieblas y trabajos, así espirituales como temporales . . . . que no basta ciencia humana para saberlo entender, ni experiencia para saberlo decir; porque sólo el que ello pasa, lo sabrá sentir, mas no decir. (qtd. in Valente, *Las palabras de la tribu* 65)

For Valente, language carries within it the duality of its insufficiency and the possibility of containing what is not explicity expressed. Valente writes of the potentiality of the word in the essay "Juan de la Cruz, el humilde del sin sentido" in *La piedra y el centro:*

> Cabría en efecto, entenderlo como afirmación implícita de la potencialidad de una palabra que, en la experiencia extrema y declarado de su radical cortedad, se constituye como espacio donde lo dicho aloja o encarna lo indecible en cuanto tal. (62)

The poetic word permits the unexpressable to exist, as indicated in the title of the poem *"Bajemos a cantar lo no cantable,"* from *Breve son* (*Punto cero* 287).

Several of Valente's texts echo the poetry of San Juan de la Cruz, in which the Spanish mystic refers to the dark night that leads to illumination on the mystic's path to union with the divine. In "Noche oscura del alma" San Juan writes, "Oh noche, que guiaste, / oh noche amable más que la alborada;" (Barnstone 309). Similar elements of the night that offers light exist in Valente's phrases "Oh luminosa noche ("Declinación de la luz," *Interior con figuras, Punto cero* 451); and "tu luminosa sombra" ("Iluminación," *Mondorla* 14); "el sol radiante de la noche" ("Antecominenzo," *Interior con figuras, Punto cero* 455); and "la aurora sólo engendrada por la noche" (untitled selection, *Material memoria, Punto cero* 462). These texts indicate the poet's search for understanding of essential principles and for revealing poetic expression. The final lines of San Juan's *El cántico espiritual* (295) appear in an untitled poem from Valente's *Material memoria:* ". . . y la caballería / a vista de las aguas descendía" (*Punto cero* 463). The corporal senses, associated with the term "caballería," undergo the purification and the spiritual renewal associated with water. Similarly, the poet searches for illumination, regeneration, and an essential totality.

A prose poem from Valente's recent collection *Mandorla* indicates that although words are not fully functioning in the capacity to express and reveal, they offer potential illumination once they emerge from a submerged state. This poem is dedicated "Al maestro cantor," as José Lezama Lima is known. The beginning and the end of the brief selection refer to the word and illumination:

> Maestro, usted dijo que en el orbe de lo poético las palabras quedan retenidas por una repentina aprehensión, destruidas, es decir, sumergidas, en un amanecer en que ellas mismas no se conocen. . . . Y no se reconoce la palabra, Palabra que habitó entre nosotros. Palabra de tal naturaleza que más que alojar el sentido, aloja la totalidad del despertar. (48)

The modifiers "retenidas," "destruidas," and "sumergidas" indicate an unrealized or an unrecognized capacity of language. The phrase "Palabra que habitó entre nosotros" echoes a Biblical text referring to the incarnation of the divine Word, Jesus Christ, who was, for the most part, not recognized as the Son of God. John 1: 10 reads, "He was in the world, the world was made by him, and the world knew him not" (111). This allusion reinforces the idea that the poetic word, although presently submerged, offers potential for enlightenment, as suggested by the verb "despertar."

Octavio Paz, in *El arco y la lira,* describes words as submerged: "Dentro, sumergidas, aguardan las palabras. Y hay que descender, ir al fondo, callar, esperar" (147-48). Valente, in "La señal," the introductory poem from *La memoria y los signos*, refers to a descent to an original "fondo," which offers a totality of meaning and expression:

> *Porque hermosa es caer, tocar el fondo oscuro*
> *donde aún se debaten las imágenes*
> *y combate el deseo con el torso desnudo*
> *la sordidez de lo vivido.*
> *Hermoso, sí.*
> *Arriba rompe el día.*
> *Aguardo sólo la señal del canto.* (*Punto cero* 147)

Valente anticipates a new dawn of poetry. The poet's search in the depths for the poetic word is also evident in Valente's "Destrucción del solitario" from *A modo de esperanza*: "Busqué en lo más hondo / la palabra" (*Punto cero* 12). The concept of searching in the depths recalls Valente's own definition of the poetic process as "un sondeo en lo oscuro" (*Las palabras de la tribu* 6) and as "un movimiento de indagación y tanteo" (7).

A selection from *Mondorla* shows the realization of the potential of the word. The transposition of a Biblical text into the poem emphasizes the creative nature of the word.

> *Momentos privilegiados en los que sobre la escritura desciende en verdad la palabra y se hace cuerpo, materia de*

85

la incarnación. Incandescente torbellino inmóvil en la ve-
locidad del centro y centro mismo de la quietud. (49)

The word is the actualizing force that endows writing with a form or body, a vital essence indicated by the terms "cuerpo" and "encarnación," echoing the Biblical passage John 1: 14: "And the word was made of flesh, and dwelt among us . . ."(111).

The dualities of movement and stillness in the words "torbellino inmóvil," "velocidad," and "quietud" call to mind Eliot's image of the Chinese jar, which "still moves perpetually in its stillness." Valente's image of the unmoving whirlwind emphasizes the duality of intense energy and tranquility, and both conditions are associated with the term "centro," suggesting unity and timelessness.

Intertextual elements related to the concept of the "center" indicate Valente's reading of the works of Mircea Eliade, scholar of religion and writer of fiction. Eliade has studied the center as "pre-eminently the zone of the sacred and the zone of absolute reality" (17). The significance of the word "center" for Valente is apparent in this poem, as well as in the title of the collection *Mondorla*, a term meaning an almond-shaped figure formed by two intersecting circles, which has a central space reserved for the Creator or a creative force (Cirlot 203). This collection of poetry emphasizes the themes of creation and creativity, the essential source of life, and illumination. In the poetic prose selection from *Mondorla*, the "word" is linked to the "center" in the sense that the incorporation of the poetic word into writing offers a revelation of some absolute reality or principle.

Valente's title *La piedra y el centro* associates the concept of the "center," symbolizing sacred space, with the image of the stone, representing totality and unity. In this collection of essays, Valente cites the words of San Juan de la Cruz, "*Como la piedra cuando se va más lle-gando a su centro . . . ,*" from the commentary in Canción XI of *El cántico espiritual* (89), to indicate an approach to the absolute, the sacred, a totality. Valente's focus on the center and the stone underscores his search for a plenitude of meaning and the revelation of the invisible through poetry. It is, in a sense, the "eternal return," to use Eliade's words.

An approach to an original totality of meaning, a universal creative principle such as the *logos*, is a major theme in Valente's work. Closely related is the subject of the poet's search for understanding of man's existence and for poetic expression. Part of Friedrich Hölderlin's question *"und wozu Dichter in dürftiger Zeit?"* ("Why poets in a time of misery?"), from *"Brot und Wein"* (Hamburger 111), appears as the epigraph to the sixth section of Valente's *La memoria y los signos (Punto cero* 197) and in the poem entitled "Poeta en tiempo de miseria" (*Punto cero* 208-09). What is the role of the poet? Hölderlin states, ". . . that which remains is established by the poets" (qtd. in Heidegger 270). Martin Heidegger, who calls Hölderlin "the poet of the poet" (271) explains Hölderlin's words in this manner: "Poetry is the establishing of being by means of the word" (281). Hölderlin also writes, "Full of merit, and yet poetically, dwells Man on this earth" (qtd. in Heidegger 270). According to Heidegger, "To 'dwell poetically' means: to stand in the presence of the gods and to be involved in the proximity of the essence of things" (282). For Valente, the poet, particularly in difficult times, is to be involved in the essence of things and to establish being and truth in his poetic word.

Textual interrelationships in the works of José ángel Valente show that his texts are significantly "traversed by otherness," in Barbara Johnson's terms. References in Valente's poetry to elements such as Eliot's "the fire and the rose," Lezama Lima's *"lo invisible,"* Zambrano's *"palabra,"* Hölderlin's *"in dürftiger Zeit*, "the "Word . . . made flesh" in Saint John, and *"no decir"* in San Juan de la Cruz energize the texts, as Johnson claims. Valente's treatment of the subject of poetry and language is enriched by the incorporation of the illuminative "words of the tribe" into his poetic word. These intertextual echoes underscore Valente's view of poetry as a process of gaining knowledge of reality, instead of a finished, unchanging product. Reality manifests itself through the act of poetic creation. The elements of intertextuality in Valente's poetry contribute to the dynamic process of *"un conocimiento 'haciéndose'"* (*Las palabras de la tribu* 7).

NOTES

[1]Valente's poetic works include *A modo de esperanza* (Madrid: Editorial Rialp. Colección Adonais, 1955); *Poemas a Lázaro* (Madrid: Indice, 1960); *Sobre el lugar del canto* (Barcelona: Colliure, 1963), an anthology of the first two publications and a final series of poems that would appear in the third major collection; *La memoria y los signos* (Madrid: Revista de occidente, 1966); *Siete representaciones* (Barcelona: El Bardo, 1967); *Breve son* (Barcelona: El Bardo, 1968); *Presentación y memorial para un monumento* (Madrid: Poesía para Todos, 1970); *El inocente* (México: Joaquín, 1970); *Punto cero (Poesía 1953-1971)* (Barcelona: Barral Editores, 1972), which includes the aforementioned individual collections; *Número trece* (Las Palmas de Gran Canaria: Inventarios Provisionales, 1972), confiscated and not in circulation; *Interior con figuras* (Barcelona: Barral Editores, 1976); *Material memoria* (Barcelona: Lay Gaya Ciencia, 1979); *Punto cero (Poesía 1953-1979)* (Barcelona: Seix Barral, 1980), which includes the aforementioned individual collections except for *Número trece*. Valente's most recent works are *Tres lecciones de tinieblas* (Barcelona: La Gaya Ciencia, 1980); *Estancias* (Madrid: Entregas de la ventura, 1980); *Sete cántigas de alén* (Sada A Coruña: Ediciós do Castro, 1981); *Noventa y nueve poemas* (Antologia), ed. José Miguel Ullán (Madrid: Alianza, 1981); *Mandorla* (Madrid: Cátedra, 1982); *El fulgor* (Madrid: Cátedra, 1984); and *Entrada en materia* (Antología), ed. Jacques Ancet (Madrid: Cátedra, 1985). Since this essay was written, Valente published another collection of poetry, *Al dios del lugar* (Barcelona:

Tusquets Editores, 1989). Valente's critical works include *Las palabras de la tribu* (Madrid: Siglo Veintiuno de España Editores, 1971), consisting of twenty-nine essays, and *La piedra y el centro* (Madrid: Taurus, 1982), containing fifteen essays oriented toward mysticism.

[2]Important studies of intertextuality in Valente's poetry include Andrew P. Debicki, "Intertextuality and Reader Response in the Poetry of José Angel Valente, 1967-1970," *Hispanic Review* 51 (Summer 1983): 251-67; Margaret H. Persin, *"José Angel Valente y la ansedad de la influencia,"* *Explicación de textos literarios* 8 (1979-80): 191-200, expanded in "José Angel Valente and the Anxiety of Influence," *Recent Spanish Poetry and the Role of the Reader* (Lewisburg: Bucknell UP, 1987): 137-51; and Santiago Daydí-Tolson, *Voces y ecos en la poesía de José Angel Valente* (Lincoln, Nebraska: Society of Spanish and Spanish-American Studies, 1984).

[3]This quotation of Valente's poetry comes from the anthology *Punto cero (Poesía 1953-1979)* (Barcelona: Editorial Seix Barral, 1980), 279. Further references to Punto cero will be given in the text.

[4]Another example of textual interrelationships in the poetry of Eliot and that of Valente, on the subject of language and poetry, is the phrase "broken images," in Eliot's "The Waste Land" (38), and "rotas imágenes," in Valente's untitled initial poem of Material memoria (Punto cero 461). Similarly, the phrase "You! hypocrite lecteur¡—mon semblable,—mon frére. " (Eliot, "The Waste Land" 39), in turn borrowed from Baudelaire's "—Hypocrite lecteur,—mon semblable, —mon frére¡" ("Au lecteur," *Les fleurs du mal, Oeuvres completes* 6), is echoed in Valente's "Retrato del autor," from El inocente: "Hasy, existe, se ha manifestado / el milagro del publico lector, / mon semblable, mon frére. / ; Hurra¡" (Punto cero 337).

[5]For an analysis of Eliot's work, see Grover Smith, *T. S. Eliot's Poetry and Plays: A Study in Sources and Meaning* (Chicago: The U of Chicago P, 1956).

WORKS CITED

Barnstone, Willis, ed. *Spanish Poetry: From Its beginnings through the Nineteenth Century.* New York: Oxford UP, 1970.

Batlló, José, ed. *Antología de la nueva poesía española.* 3rd ed. Barcelona: Editorial Lumen, 1977.

Baudelaire, Charles. *Oeuvres complètes.* France: Gallimard, 1975.

Bosley, Keith, ed. and trans. *Mallarmé: The Poems.* England: Penguin Books, 1977.

Cirlot, J. E. *A Dictionary of Symbols.* 2nd ed. Trans. Jack Sage, New York: The Philosophical Library, 1971; rpt. 1983.

Daydí-Tolson, Santiago. *Voces y ecos en la poesía de José Angel Valente.* Lincoln, Nebraska: Society of Spanish and Spanish-American Studies, 1984.

Debicki, Andrew P. "Intertextuality and Reader Response in the Poetry of José Angel Valente, 1967-1970." *Hispanic Review* 51 (Summer 1983): 251-67.

Eliade, Mircea. *The Myth of the Eternal Return: Or, Cosmos and History.* Trans. Willard R. Trask. Princeton: Princeton UP, 1965.

Elito, T. S. *The Complete Poems and Plays: 1909-1950.* San Diego: Harcourt Brace Jovanovich, 1971.

Hamburger, Michael, ed. *Hölderlin.* Baltimore: Penguin, 1961

Heidegger, Martin *Existence and Being.* Ed. Werner Brock. Chicago: Henry Regnery Company, 1949.

Holy Bible. New Jersey: Thomas Nelson Inc., 1972.

Johnson, Barbara. *A World of Difference.* Baltimore: The Johns Hopkins UP, 1987.

Juan de la Cruz, San. *El cántico espiritual.* Ed. M. Martínez Burgos. Madrid: Espasa-Calpe, 1952.

Paz, Octavio. *El arco y la lira: El moema. La revelación poética. Poesía e historia.* 2nd ed. México: Fondo de Cultura Económica, 1970.

Persin, Margaret H. " José Angel Valente y la ansiedad de la influencia." *Explicación de textos literarios* 8 (1979-80): 191-200.

_____. *Recent Spanish Poetry and the Role of the Reader.* Lewisburg: Bucknell UP, 1987.

Smith, Grover, ed. *T. S. Eliot's Poetry and Plays: A Study in Sources and Meaning.* Chicago: The U of Chicago P, 1956.

Valente. José Angel. *Breve son.* Barcelona: El Bardo, 1968.

_____. *El fulgor.* Madrid: Cátedra, 1984.

_____. *El inocente.* México: Joaquín Mortiz, 1970

_____. *Interior con figuras.* Barcelona: Barral, 1976.

_____. *La memoria y los signos.* Madrid: Revista de occidente, 1966.

_____. *La piedra y el centro.* Madrid: Taurus, 1982.

_____. *Las palabras de la tribu.* Madrid: Siglo Veintiuno de España, 1971.

_____. *Mandorla.* Madrid: Cátedra, 1982.

_____. *Material memoria.* Barcelona: La Gaya Ciencia, 1979.

_____. *Punto cero: (Poesía 1953-1979).* Barcelona: Seix Barral, 1980.

Zambrano, María. *Claros del bosque.* Barcelona: Seix Barral, 1977.

_____. *El sueño creador. Obras reunidas.* Madrid: Aguilar, 1971.

8.   PLACING SOURCE IN *GREED* AND *MCTEAGUE*

Mary Lawlor

THE FETISHIZATION OF GOLD among the characters in Frank Norris's 1899 novel *McTeague* is an expression of profound respect for an object that operates in the text as the very image of signification, the source of possibility for endless exchanges that reverberate beyond the immediately economic. In almost any culture, gold is what we might call the ultimate signifier: it can mean whatever you can substitute it for, and you can, theoretically, substitute it for anything. As embodiment of such potential, gold functions as a standard, an authority whose value is self-evident and determines that of other things for which it can be exchanged. Thus it circulates through *McTeague* as the mark of meaning itself, an extended metaphor for the system of references and associations that constitute the very process of narration. But within the narrative economy that it engenders, gold comes to participate as simply one of the many elements that perpetuate desire.[1]

Gold, the valuable stuff hidden in the earth, has no inherent worth, or in any case, very little practical use in Norris's time. In its culturally-determined capacity to be exchanged for anything and in its lack of inherent value, gold poses a very magnified paradigm of the associative exchange values of all objects in conscious and unconscious activity, demonstrating in bright terms that things in themselves signify nothing, but take their price from the values of other things for which they may, for whatever reasons, be made to substitute. This frankly semiotic lesson that gold offers is rehearsed regularly through *McTeague* and demonstrates Norris's peculiar habit of playing with signs, marks, the hoaxes in words and the *trompe l'oeil* in pictures, as if the signifier itself were the object of his interest and ridicule.[2]

On the other hand, the image of gold cast by culture has much to do with matter. Embedded in earth, it is after all a mineral one desires to touch—the object towards which the miner's search is directed. The abstract issues of signification and meaning leave the rock cold, in an orthodox Naturalist sense; but just as Naturalism creates its own romanticism in order to repress it, gold's authority is diminished by the very fact of an argument in the free silver-gold standard debates of the 1890s, only to retain its mythical value in the nostalgic adoration of a once stable convention. The lack of inherent value discussed above is one thing; but the residue of gold's value-in-itself, accumulated through long centuries of western culture, permits it to be fetishized and to retain its respect in the face of its arbitrary value; thus it becomes an emblem of pure essence, highly placed, tangible, and signifying nothing. The excessive materiality in this understanding of gold, considered in contrast with the excessive abstraction of its role as infinite signifier, gives its figure a certain androgynous shape. The metaphor holds not only to the combination of female matter and phallic signification, but the promiscuity of the body as signifier in the figure of the androgyne. Thus we have in the metal a combination of traditional gender notations, a merging of parent functions in one fertile and potent thing. The stasis and internal locus associated with gold-as-essence keep it rooted, in place and steady: an icon of stability. The promiscuity and ejaculation of meaning available to it as capital signifier indicate movement, desire, fluctuation. The realm of gold-as-essence is place; of gold-as-signifier, time. The two references, simultaneous in the image or word of gold, draw the miner's attention as object and subject in one. As object of the search, it is held in awe; as reflection of the possibilities for exchange, it becomes a model of subjectivity. In the split figure of felicity and significations, it is as if the gold served as a reverberating place in which a desire is perceived that the seeker takes for their own.[3]

This brief allegory of gold as model signifier and as pure matter that becomes subsumed in the system of exchanges which it produces is repeated in the function of the mute true West and its "Life" as source in Norris's aesthetics of literary representation.[4] The same respect for, and sublimation of source, appears in von Stroheim's adaptation of the novel in *Greed*. For all three of these relations, the privileged authority which speaks for its own value is sought as parent for the production that follows it. But as causes of desire, these engendering objects take their places within the narrative economies rather than remaining outside as privileged forbears. Thus, the idea of the unmediated true West is embedded in Norris's landscapes—urban and wild—and character descriptions as a source which cannot be obtained; similarly, the novel itself is enmeshed in von Stroheim's adaptation as an origin to which the film cannot be faithful. Nonetheless, in all three cases, the seeker studies and courts the origin in an attempt to be faithful to its value, but succeeds rather in possessing the idealized source by appropriating it for something different.

The Western landscape that mutely informs much of Norris's imagination causes him often to back away from his writing, to check and re-state his aesthetic claims and his prose style. Parody abounds in his work in a microscopic version of loss and recuperation of the writer's integrity in the face of a too-writerly passage he has written. Of course, the representation which he attempts to make so faithful and adequate to the West is another set of literary conventions, which are abhorred in his desire to be original to a unique reality; and the incessant Norris anxiety of writing spills all over the page. We know that he knows that none of his marks is anything but a belated pose, part of a repertoire of possible expressions that ineptly follows from the ideal of plenty in the possibilities he imagines when looking at, for example, the Sierra Nevada, Death Valley, the expanse of the Mojave Desert. The respect that these places inspire is for something ancient and simultaneously new in the fleeting moment of the gazer's experience; and the representation fabricates its anxiety by speaking the old and the new at once.

In 1897, Norris wrote, addressing himself to young writers "Give us stories now . . . with red hot blood . . . with unleased passions rampant. . . . Think of the short stories that are happening every hour of the time. It's the life that we want, the vigorous real thing, not the curious weaving of words and the polish of literary finish . . ." (Pizer, 30). Concerning his ideals of realism in relation to *Greed*, von Stroheim wrote, "I was going to film stories which would be life-like to the Nth degree. I intended to show men and women as they are all over the world...their good and bad qualities, their noble...and their jealous, vicious, mean and greedy sides" (Finler, 7). both artists claim a distaste for design and theory in favor of the spontaneous impulses of "life." But this is itself a position, a theory, and it relies on a certain limited range of artistic conventions in order to support itself—largely a mode we call Realism, or its relative, Naturalism.

The novel's division between the two very different dramatic situations of the urban-domestic and the wilderness scenarios provides certain of the characters alternate levels on which to act out their avarice. Given Norris's general and overt emphasis on what he tries to know in an immediate way as "life"—the rough and raw realism of the West—we might reasonably consider the two situations as separate fields of value-determination that the novel compares. The late mining sequence, for example, takes the problem of greediness back to money's source in the bowels of the Sierra Nevada, the privileged place of McTeague's own origins. Mining itself, a more blatant way of pursuing gold than the complicated mechanisms of urban social exchange and the guile of the bank, is presented here as if it were a more primary and simple model by which to study the relation of the human psyche to the metal it has made precious. In this scenario, the relation is more properly speaking greed—the desire for something one does not yet have—than the avarice we find in Trina's behavior concerning her coined gold.

In both the novel and the original film versions of the story, McTeague and Cribbens discuss approaches to mining before they set out prospecting. Cribbens has been exposed to a lot of talk on the subject, and he has made himself something of a geologist by reading about it and prospecting in rather a "scientific manner": "Shucks...Gi'me a long distinct contact between sedimentary igneous rocks, an' I'll sink a shaft without ever seeing 'color.'"(223)[5]

McTeague denies the value of any theoretical approach and simply responds, "Gold is where you find it." The difference between the two approaches centers on the issue of interpretation. Cribbens's idea requires that the prospector read the landscape for indications of material that cannot be seen on the surface. The contact of igneous and sedimentary rock signifies the possibility of quartz, which is in turn a clue to the invisible presence of gold. McTeague thinks that such codification of the ground is useless: one might find gold at such a point, and one might not. The dentist "clung to the old prospector's idea that there was no way of telling where gold was until you actually saw it." Rather than proceeding by Cribbens's conventions, which not only describe a certain meaning to the terrain, but create that meaning in Cribbens's almost sentimental fondness for the terms of his theory, McTeague will simply take things as they come and avoid such a representative approach to the land (223).

His slogan, "Gold is where you find it," suggests the ideal, spontaneous realism of "Life" in Norris's aesthetics of fiction; but afterall, it is a theory founded on ideological and psychological pressures. McTeague is a dumb hero, and the simplicity of his method here is entirely appropriate to his character. Nonetheless, the character utters Norris's realism; and Cribbens, the more intelligent of the two, is made to seem, at moments, more interpretive, or conscious of style and design than the author's aesthetics would overtly approve. The expression of his theory quoted above smacks of Norris's habit of parodying Western speakers, with the incongruous combination of slang and scientific discourse. So we have the impression that Cribbens's stylized methodology is a violation of the pure Western experience embodied in McTeague's aphorism, and that his character is something of a joke. But several pages further, Cribbens's description of the correct context for gold matches precisely the geological configurations of the spot where the discovery occurs. The argument, however, is still unsettled since all we have here is one incident, and certainly McTeague's tautology cannot be denied.

The parody of representation posed here in the form of Cribbens's prospecting echoes the general anxiety about writing that appears throughout Norris's work. A method like Cribbens's is by definition necessary, although Norris would rather sanction the immediacy of McTeague's idea by enacting it in writing. but the latter enactment instantly puts the work back into Cribbens's camp. The kind of rock which the image in this section of the story employs, the igneous granodiorite and the sedimentary slate, combine forces internal and external to the specific location where they lie, and the product of this interaction is the gold—the essential meaning behind the geological signifiers in Cribbens's interpretation. Against this neat equation, Norris's aesthetics, fighting to diminish the internal, projective vision of the convention-filled writerly imagination, attempt to register a primarily external impression of the real. The image of the two kinds of rock, igneous, the more or less inherent to the spot where it is found; and sedimentary, which has in a sense settled or slid in from elsewhere, stands as a neat little code for the ideal production of meaning, a meeting of subjectivity and objectivity that is not, afterall, pure subjective hoax.

The issue of signification and meaning is played out in the treatment of the landscape as a text to be interpreted or not to be interpreted, in the same vein as the discussion of the value of gold. Norris's frequent anxiety concerning the propriety of writing emphasizes his distrust for the signifier, a wariness of any mark's pretension to "stand for" something else and its inevitable self reference, or rhetorical guise. But the distrust seems to eventuate in a perverse fetishization of the signifier as such, the same kind of background-less obsession that we see in Trina's, Mac's and Zerkow's lust for gold.

As early as 1906, von Stroheim had expressed a wish to film *McTeague.* What he produced was a very lengthy, visual translation of the book—in effect a cinema novel. He claimed artistic principles that duplicate Norris's and even went so far as to use some of Norris's statements on realism in the film's introduction. In his wish to respect and to preserve the authenticity of *McTeague*, von Stroheim organized a series of production methods that stressed his idea of a faithful adaptation. He filmed on location, without using a single studio set, and required his principal actors to sleep in the house where most of the early portions of the story were filmed, so that they could "really feel 'inside' the characters they were to portray" (Finler, 29). Much of his working script attempts a page for page transcription of the novel.

Von Stroheim stressed what he perceived as his fidelity to Norris in comments written much later: "I was given *plein pouvoir* to make the picture as the author might have wanted it"; and he complains that Louis Mayer and Irving Thalberg of MGM "did not care a hoop about what the author or I . . . had wanted" (Finler, 28). The epigraph from Norris's essay "The True Reward of the Novelist" (Pizer, 87) that opens the film appears in von Stroheim's foreword to Peter Noble's *Hollywood Scapegoat: The Biography of Erich von Stroheim* with minor alterations and no credit to Norris (xiii). The impression that it is von Stroheim's own statement blurs the influence in a way that is at once utter fidelity, in the sense that von Stroheim speaks Norris's words without declaring a difference between the two voices; and plain theft. The simultaneous acts of love and violation in this citation are symptomatic of the playful fidelity that operates throughout the adaptation.

One of the major differences between the film's structure and that of the novel lies in point of view. The signly character of Norris's novel makes itself known in the collection of photographs, emblems, certificates, coins, signs, written announcements and so forth. But the steady pressure of McTeague's angle of vision in the narrative perspective suggests the thinness of the entire story itself, that is, its status as an elaborate emblem surrounding the arch emblem gold, whose referent to some reality is sheer illusion. There is something solipsistic and degenerate in the narrow channel of McTeague's point of view which to a great extent controls the narrative scope; elements of story are chosen from the realm of possibilities by McTeague's position. The psychology of Norris's work is in its narrative structure: its angling and its paced repetitions, which function as rhythmic obsessions.

Von Stroheim's camera relieves the pressure of McTeague's perspective in the novel and distributes it among the principals, which results in a more naturalistic narrative manipulation, recording all of their actions as if it were a voyeur of their foolishness, not granting the special or privileged and thus romantic quality to the movement of McTeague's vision. The absence of this particularized scope deflates the obsessive looking that expresses McTeague's desire in the novel and replaces it with a general desire on the part of the camera to look, and to see the corners of human character normally hidden in early cinema. This is von Stroheim's 'realism.'

The play of the camera across the whole field of characters, set and landscape, does not thereby achieve the supposed disinterest of the naturalist force[6]—the sort of unresponsive objectivity that would ideally leave the world cold in the literary scene. The camera makes its choices from moment to moment, and the sequence, the juxtapositions, angles and depths of shots constitute a perspective, and necessarily an interest. The subjectivity operating is that of von Stroheim and his cameramen William Daniels and Ben Reynolds, enabled by the object *McTeague* which resists their pure projection in the same way that they resist the extended projection of any one of the characters' perspectives.

Distribution of point of view has a strong effect on the logic of the story, since it means that McTeague's stupidity is not the determining movement. In Norris, the tale moves lyrically at points, particularly in the descriptive passages of setting and landscape; but its epistemology is slow, full of gaps, as piecemeal as McTeague's capacity to understand. *Greed* indulges itself in a plethora of information to comment, explain, identify an action, or a character's condition in a way that the novel often refuses.

Von Stroheim's backgrounds and causes, on the other hand, are elaborated in full visual drama. His is a more linear, logical progression. From the Big Dipper opening we witness the behavior of figures who are overtly presented as sources of McTeague's own character—the drinking father who beats and neglects a pining, money-searching wife. The use of irises and barn-doors in the movement from sequence to sequence emphasizes von Stroheim's assumption of narrative linkage and cohesion, like a series of doors or apertures that open and close, announcing time in the endings and beginnings of things. The progressions from distant shots to close ups is related to this sense of sequencing. The film starts with an iris on the Big Dipper Gold Mine: "A tree covered mountain with the mine building in the distance."

> Medium shot of the mine building with its chimney smoking
> Medium long shot inside the building, of a giant ore-crushing machine in operation . . .
> Close-up of one section of the machine working.
> Close-up of hands shovelling a muddy-looking substance with a trowel . . .
> Medium long shot of various men working in the mine (Finler, 37).

The set of commands intends to direct the crew's and the viewer's attention to a linear progression from external to interior acquaintance with the scene. Through a step by step display of the environment, the settlement and the workings of the mine we are made intimate not only with all of the data that von Stroheim wants us to have in order to situate the story; but with the signifying reverberations of machine, industry, digging, interiority, repetition. The mechanical operations in the interior shots, following the idyllic pastoral of the opening iris suggest one of the story's lessons in signification: the outer sweetness contains an inner mechanical obsession, greedy and stupid. McTeague's figure compares nicely with the equation. Thus von Stroheim provides an easier link between signification and meaning than Norris does, even as the relation between inner and outer in relation to meaning is itself a typical Norris lesson in the difficulties of signification. The linking mechanisms of von Stroheim's story-telling project a desire to explain that is unabashed in comparison with Norris's.

The narrative hiatuses in the novel beg commentary, some sort of effective analysis or identification from the narrator, which is denied. The reader is led from one traumatic moment to the next, and potential sympathy is often exploited in parody. Trina's amputated fingers mark a great change in her condition, which rather than being in any empathic way accounted for, is treated by the following comment: "One can hold a scrubbing-brush with two good fingers and the stumps of two others even if both joints of the thumb are gone, but it takes considerable practice to get used to it" (271).

The gaps in narration and resistance of sympathy have an effect of fragmentation on sections of the novel, so that it often reads in a rather reportorial style, accountable enough by reference to Norris's experiences in journalism, but its affinity with the strong consciousness of representation of the American 1890s allows us to read a sensibility in it that comes close to what we call post-modernism. Von Stroheim's piece, chronologically more "modern" than Norris's, contains a more Victorian logic. We might hypothesize that his lengthy exposure to the fiction of Prussian gallantry and the very lively way that he moved, as director, among the tangible dimensions of these sentimental stories of gentility[7] infected his narratology with the explanatory habits that we find in *Greed*.

In Norris, the gaps suggest that objects do not safely signify anything: they simply reflect each other and do not refer with realistic integrity, beyond this play. but to say this is also to imply the simultaneous sadness and humor that Norris's naturalism imposes on its meaningless conditions, an implication of a sure sense of reference. Von Stroheim's story changes this avant-garde sensibility and recasts that game of signification into a story-teller' s story, where every dramatic moment is enlisted to participate in the delivery of a traditional narrative logic. *Greed*, however, directs its references not to money or mining or marriage as they are found in an actual world, but to the representations of these things in *McTeague*. Like the miner questing for the mother lode and the author for the nugget of true depiction, von Stroheim's film plays between receptivity to "what is there" and interpretive projection, between fidelity and violation in the desire to place its source.

NOTES

[1] For a similar discussion of gold as the incarnation of the "economic principle of substitution and replacement" and its gender-inflected ways of producing meaning in Balzac, see Felman, 37-39.

[2] Michael's title chapter on Norris provides a very interesting and instructive discussion of the question of value in several fields of representation during the American 1890's, particularly in relation to money.

[3] This discussion has much in common with Felman's reading of Balzac's "The Girl With the Golden Eyes," but there gold's double function of signifier and signified is understood as ultimately representative of male desire.

[4] For a discussion of the term "Life" in Norris's criticism, see Pizer, xiii-xxii. The same respect and sublimation of source appears in von Stroheim's adaptation of the novel in *Greed.*

[5] This and subsequent citations of *McTeague* are taken from the Norton Critical Edition, edited by Donald Pizer (1977).

[6]For a comprehensive and very useful history of this term and the ideas attached to it in nineteenth-century American writing, see Martin.

[7]Koszarski's biography presents a full study of the construction of the on and off screen von Stroheim personæ through his many films.

WORKS CITED

Felman, Shoshana. "Reading Femininity." *Yale French Studies* 62 (1981): 19-44.

Finler, Joel, ed. *Greed: A Film by Erich von Stroheim.* New York: Simon and Schuster. 1972.B

Koszarski, Richard. *The Man You Loved to Hate: The Biography of Erich von Stroheim.* New York: Oxford University Press, 1983.B

Martin, Ronald. *American Literature and the Universe of Force.* Durham, N.C.: Duke University Press, 1981.

Michaels, Walter Benn. *The Gold Standard and the Logic of Naturalism.* Berkeley, Calif.: University of California Press, 1987.

Noble, Peter. *Hollywood Scapegoat: The Biography of Erich von Stroheim.* New York: Arno Press, 1972.

Norris, Frank. *McTeague.* New York: Norton, 1977.

Pizer, Donald *The Literary Criticism of Frank Norris.* Austin: University of Texas Press, 1964..

9. DESICA'S *BICYCLE THIEVES* AND THE ATTACK ON THE CLASSICAL HOLLYWOOD FILM

Gerard Molyneaux

IN THE OPENING SCENE OF Vittorio DeSica's *Bicycle Thieves* (1949) the hero, Antonio Ricci, is tracked to by the camera and discovered lying on the grass. Now alerted by a friend, he runs to the employment agent and learns that his two years of unemployment may be over. He has a job! He will work for the city pasting up posters on the walls of Rome. That choice of jobs for the hero is eccentric in a variety of ways. First, Antonio Ricci, prior to this calling, has no experience as a bill poster, nor, at this point, does he own the bike necessary to get him around the city. Second, the later narrative fails to justify by development the seeming arbitrariness of the job assignment since Ricci never gets beyond hanging one poster. The capriciousness of the story is further accentuated by the formal intrusion of film images within the film: because of Ricci's work, the viewer, at least for a time, will be exposed to reminders of the film world beyond the world of the film's story.

Admittedly, *Bicycle Thieves* is a traditional narrative of the relationship of father and son. Therefore, the potentially distracting or distancing effects that these film images might cause in the viewer raise questions concerning the possible reasons for the DeSica's selecting a film-centered job and about how the spectator might read this part of the film's text. A search for the source of DeSica's inspiration leads to two sets of relationships: that of the movie to its fictional source, the novel by Luigi Bartolini, and that between film and the Italian (Roman) society of 1948. What kind of correspondence existed between the hero of the novel and Antonio Ricci in the film? What kind of interaction was transpiring between the Italian film system and the economic and social world in which it functioned? Further, witnessing these pictures of American and Italian films within *Bicycle Thieves*, what kind of dual or triple attitude must the viewer today adopt to decode their meanings?

Literary reviews offer little inducement for further serious consideration of the Bartolini novella as a privileged source for the film. Most critics dismiss it quickly. Ostensibly however, DeSica seems quite generous in acknowledging his debt to "this remarkable writer who, with his vivid style, has given me inspirational motivation for my new film" ("Why..." 87). On the other hand, his claim that he would simply find "an idea and a title for a film from it" understates his indebtedness in that it leaves unmentioned the many other similarities between the film and its source ("What..." 87). Possibly because the novel was neither popular nor critically well received, contemporary and later film critics have accepted too readily DeSica's low estimate of its influence. For example, by way of footnote, film critic and historian Mira Liehm concludes, "Bartolini's well-written but rather mediocre book provided the film with just the title and the basic plot" (Liehm 75). In fact, the sharing of the title, however, seems more ironic than imitative since in the novel, "The Bicycle Thieves" conveys the narrator's arrogance toward the rabble while in the film these same words suggest the shared plight of the hero with the other poor outcasts that populate the story. The playful adaptation of the title aside, the fact is DeSica's film has turned to Bartolini's book for more than an idea or plot—or title.

Structurally, both the film and the novel employ the classical unities of time, place, and action. The events occur over a three day period (Friday to Sunday) in post-World War II Rome. In each work, the quest to recover the stolen bike takes the reader/viewer to actual locations with references to the same neighborhoods and streets. Likewise, many of the institutions and personnel cited in the novel are also visited in the film: police station, church, and whore houses. Admittedly, these places and types would be the common targets of many of the "neorealist" works; nevertheless, they suggest the filmmaker's reliance on this source. Specifically the film sometimes simply borrows, and at other times adapts details from, Bartolini's book. In both works, for example, three thieves steal the bike with one of them pointing the pursuing hero in the wrong direction. Further details corroborate the allegiance of film to novel as, for instance, when subsequently the thieves remove a dent from the frame and paint over the bike. Even the villain remains unaltered in the transition from print to picture. The primary suspect is a twenty-year old thief who is saved from prosecution by the fact that he has epilepsy. The memorable film image of the little boy halting the father's pursuit of the thief and peeing in the street also appears first in the novel.

This listing of borrowings, and it is abbreviated rather than exhaustive here, suggests that the novel was then a much-employed source for the film's action, characters, and story details. On seeing the film, however, Bartolini responded with a "violent protest about the treatment of his material" (Armes 151). Despite the author's objections, the film has faithfully preserved much more of the book than has been heretofore acknowledged. Yet for all the adoption of details, and reworking similar characters and narrative events, the film remains *dramatically* different from its source.

When DeSica chose to alter in a radical way the nature of the hero from Tory to peasant, his decision determined a narrative and a set of themes clearly at odds with those found in the book. The first-person and stridently omniscient narrator of the novel is as experienced, opinionated, and feisty as the film's Antonio Ricci is innocent, mute, and passive. Evidently a man of means, the author-artist hero of the novel pursues the stolen bike on his back-up bike. Perhaps it is this profligacy of vehicles that accounts for his penchant for forgetting about the chase and launching into long digressions about the intrigue, graft and corruption that comprise life in post-war Rome. He is a conceited crank who loses track of his story and finally becomes tiresome (*Canadian Forum*, 31). Tedious though the narrator may be, his commentary does provide for the reader who has seen the film the kind of background that puts into historical perspective and helps to explain the events, images, and allusions found in the movie. Conversely, through the journey of the hero, DeSica's film dramatizes the kinds of inhumanity the novel's voice so often describes and condemns.

Unlike the Bartolini's wealthy bachelor-hero who seems to pursue the stolen bike for the sake of principle, the film's Antonio Ricci must track down the bike because his life and his family depend on it. Paradoxically, Ricci's work will at the same time perpetuate, through the posters, a fantasy of success far removed from the actualities of his streets. In three ways, the film poster-hanging job dramatizes the difference between the "haves" and "have-nots:" within the framework of film as art, as socioeconomic system, and as cultivator of a culture. Both as viewer and voyeur, the spectator is involved in the triple dialectical opposition of Rita Hayworth to Antonio Ricci, of Hollywood to Rome, and of independent Italian film and classical Hollywood narrative movie. Nothing in Bartolini's novel suggests the richness that DeSica's film conveys in its use of film as metonymic symbol.

The radical departure from the novel found in the filmmaker's choice of work for the hero and in his motivation for finding the bike excite a need for considering the implications and consequences of these narrative decisions. Moreover, novel aside, the use of the film-related job and its attached symbols is not casual. They are found in a film produced with extraordinary attention to the details of structure and the refinements of text. Here neorealism does not mean offhand or cheap; on the contrary over the years the realism of *Bicycle Thieves* seems increasingly the product of careful manipulation of the film and of audience. There are, for example, the almost minutely drawn parallels and reversals in the fortunes of father and son and the inventive use of psychologically plausible motivation (when the downtrodden father suddenly takes his son out for dinner). Further, this film about the streets of Rome is haunted by very dreamlike apparitions of the thief and of the German seminarians. The rightness of these other choices throughout the film argues for an assessment of the impact of film imagery in DeSica's movie. Since the answer for its use does not lie in the novel, one turns elsewhere. What was happening in postwar Italy that would impel a filmmaker to use the icons of his art in his art? How was film interacting with the society, with Italian social and legal institutions, and with world-wide systems of filmmaking? How were the crises faced by a filmmaker comparable to those determining the lives of those people in the audience? Most importantly this paper would ask: What stance does *Bicycle Thieves* take toward the classical Hollywood film, toward its ideology, and toward Hollywood itself?

At the time of *Bicycle Thieves'* production, DeSica was working with the most overly determined of the media and in a socio-political environment bent on imposing even more rules, moral codes, and laws on the cinema. As Robert Ray observes, "...cinema exists in a dense shifting network of relationships with other processes...specifically as a technologically dependent, capital intensive, commercial, collaborative medium regulated by the government and financially indebted to mass audiences...."(p. 8). In postwar Italy, the film system worked in the interest of the government, which in turn was beholden to the United States. Filmmakers then were responsive to both governments and, by extension, to the film system most congenial with the myths and ideology of the United States, namely, the classical Hollywood film. During the war, that system of film had been sustained in Italy by the Psychological Warfare Branch of the American Army ensuring, even in

1943, a massive importation and exhibition of American films (Debrecz 7).

Symptomatic of what happened after the war was the opening in Naples of the Metropolitan Theatre. Once a cave used as an air-raid shelter, the Metropolitan went into business by premiering not an Italian film but Hollywood's *Ali Baba and the Forty Thieves*. "On Sundays peasant women swarm in from the island and from the mainland down the bay" (Genet, 3/12/49 p. 66). Throughout the late forties, the American films dominated the Italian screen. From 1947 to 1950, nearly seventy percent of the films shown were American; only ten percent were Italian-produced (Leihm, 331). Certainly the backlog of American films unseen during the war helps to account for this saturation by the Hollywood studios, and as Bondonella indicates, "Most Italians preferred the Hollywood products and native Italian farces and historical dramas" (Bondanella, 36). The audience preference, coupled with the political and economic dependence of Italy on the United States, perpetuated Hollywood's domination of the Italian screen and helped to stifle the voices of change both social and cinematic. Writing of neorealist films, Borde notes: "The clerical offensive, the sharpening of censorship, the growing power of the Christian Democrats over the life of the country, all played a major role...But the immediate cause was financial, the films on social themes did not make money; or at least, they did not make enough money" (Huaco, 189).

Controlling the American money that arrived for the European Recovery Act (The Marshall Plan), the government diverted funding away from any production that "might have mobilized the left into a counter cinema" (Silverman, 41). In consort with the government itself were the remnants of the Fascists who controlled the studio production facilities and who insured "a deliberate blocking of production money...until such time as any money could be safely invested in an ideologically 'stable' product" (Silverman, 40). If the economic stranglehold would not discourage a filmmaker, censorship would. Those who did not toe the ideological line were condemned for disloyalty to their country, as DeSica was for his depiction of prison life in *Shoeshine*. The officials of the Department of Ministry did not say that what he had shown was false. Rather as Chiaromonte says in referring to that film which was set in a prison for children, "They said it was a smear of Italy's honor" (Huaco, 169). Stultifyingly in tandem with the government was the Catholic Church, which in *Osservatore Romano* would later attack *Bicycle Thieves'* depiction of a Catholic charity as showing, (again Chiaromonte's observation) "only the dingy side of things" (Huaco 179). On political and moral bases then, all films, domestic and foreign, were subject to censorship. Under that wide umbrella came any showing of the country in a negative way. These films would be denied the right of export for showings, especially in America. Consequently filmmakers were pressed into self-censoring their own films. "Since domestic consumption could never generate enough revenues to meet neorealist production costs, the refusal of access to foreign markets was a sure promise of financial failure. Those who persevered in making neorealist films did so at great financial risk, as Vittorio DeSica was quick to point out" (Marcus, 27).

In regard to the question of censorship of the Italian films, the worker's job as a bill-poster in DeSica's movie seems especially pointed for not only were scripts and movies censored, so were the posters that advertised them. Argeo Santucci noted, "The censorship is extended even to posters and other advertising materials" (Huaco, 193). The vigilance with which these film posters were censored seems to be reflected in the kind of and style of poster that Ricci is mounting in *Bicycle Thieves*. The poster shows Rita Hayworth posed like the nightclub singer in *Gilda* (1946), draped in black, her arms outspread singing about "putting the blame on Mame." The alluring and sexually suggestive quality of the image is mitigated by the white band of print pasted over her thighs. That the wide strip of print may allude to the standard operating procedure at work here can be verified by the description of Italian movie posters at the time. "Prior to the banning of Botticelli, the government required Roman movie posters of no more than ordinary commercial daring to be bandaged with strips of paper which, in most cases, turned out to be little signs saying 'Great Success' or 'Closing Soon" wittily pasted over the star's bosom or knees...."(Genet 7/9/49 p.40). This poster's band simply says, "Hayworth."

Any independent Italian filmmaker in the forties had to buck or knuckle under to the systems of film imposed by the Italian and the American studios. According to Raymond Borde, many were discouraged by the economic and censorship constraints and, "abandoned those film projects closest to their hearts" (Huaco, 189). DeSica was one of the others who overcame the discouragements. Initially he found little interest in this simple film about an unemployed worker who loses his bike. Described by Bazin as a story having the interest of a lost dog column, the plot was well removed from the classical Hollywood product, especially in its lack of stars and unhappy ending without closure. Stylistically too, the proposed film would depart measurably from "that prevalent in the 'white telephone' films of Fascist Italy" and most glamorous Hollywood products (Overby, 13).

DeSica himself seems like the most unlikely of candidates for the role of independent filmmaker resisting the blandishments of Hollywood and the constraints of Italian film production. From his roots he was a performer who emerged from the most orthodox entertainment tradition and training in Italy. Primarily he played romantic leads on the stage and in films which he viewed "merely as a means of making money" (Liehm, 46). His post-war flirtation with realism is an anomalous chapter in a career as star, director, and producer whose work was primarily given over to entertaining, not evaluating social crises or educating his audience. Even his neorealist films were more like Chaplin and Dickens than like communist or socialist tracts. His films did, however, depict divorce, suicide and the suffering of children, and those were events proscribed in the Italian cinema prior to the war. In *Bicycle Thieves* he produced a film about a man on the dole. Only in a country where unemployment was never shown on screen would this film seem radical. (Liehm, 56). As Ranieri observes, "The bottom line of the film, and to the shame of certain declarations against the same director, is this: that the Italy of 1948 is a country of the bicycle, but Ricci does not have his own bicycle as ten years before Italy was the country of the white telephone, but people did not have white telephones" (303).

In proposing *The Bicycle Thieves,* DeSica was exercising his neorealist view that "a good film must reflect the country of its origins" (Samuels, 144). Neither the Italian producers nor the public, however, seemed attracted to a film without beautiful people doing romantic things. DeSica therefore turned to Hollywood for help. Of all the possible American producers, only David O. Selznick saw potential success in the project—provided one adjustment was made: Cary Grant would star in the role of the worker. DeSica declined, and his reasons for resisting Selznick's offer suggest the difference between the kinds of determination bearing on a classical Hollywood film and those operating in a neorealist film production. "I needed a man who eats like a worker, who can bring himself to cry, who bats his wife around and expresses his love for her by slamming her on the shoulder, the buttocks, the head. Cary Grant isn't used to doing such things, and he can't do them. Therefore Selznick refused the money" (Samuels, 147).

Eventually DeSica found other sources to finance what was, as both Peter Bondanella and Mira Liehm have argued, an elaborate professional attempt to convey realism. In light of the opposition posed by the film industries, his scrapes with censorship from the church and government, and his conflict with Selznick's taste, DeSica's choice of jobs for his hero begins to seem less and less arbitrary and more and more suggestive a point of view on the tension between classical Hollywood (Italian white-telephone) and neorealist visions of reality and film. An examination of the way in which the film's narrative presents and develops the career of Ricci as film poster hanger would suggest that rather than being incidental to the story, the job is the focal point around which is built an attack on the classical film's formal style, structural fixtures, and perpetuated myths. From the opening scenes of the film until the bike stealing sequence, the film builds to a classical climax only to frustrate it with the intrusion of neorealist fact. In *The Bicycle Thieves,* Hollywood seems hoisted on its own petard. The film uses that favorite thematic paradigm of displacing onto the hero the socioeconomic problems of a whole society to be dealt with within that "ideologically favored realm of melodrama" (Ray, 13). Then, with the stealing of the bike, the film debunks that whole comforting formula in favor of a less predictable, less linear, and more discursive film.

The eventual dismissal of the classical Hollywood formula-centered plot is carefully prepared for through the dialectical interaction of it with the more open, less tidy, and symbol laden narrative of *Bicycle Thieves.* On the one hand, the plot is propelling the audience toward the Hollywood closure; on the other, the actors, the camera work, symbols, and the mise-en-scène are stalling, disrupting, and working independently from the propulsion of the plot. The structure of this first quarter of the film invites the audience to take part in a narrative formula standardized in the classical film (Bordwell, 6). The scenario prescribes that the hero pursue both a practical goal and a woman and that the attaining of the goal will in the end unite him with the woman. Whatever the genre—western, spy, war film—the action follows the same kind of reassuring pattern described by the heroine in Wood Allen's *Purple Rose of Cairo* who relates to her sister the plot ascribable to so many Hollywood films: "It's about a taxi driver who becomes a radio star and then an opera singer." Classical Hollywood film fitted the myth of American individual enterprise into a "rigorous chain of cause and effect" (Bordwell, 16). Ostensibly *Bicycle Thieves* seems bent on following the lead of the Hollywood film. In DeSica's film, the hero must get a job to restore life to his family. But to get the job, he must first overcome the obstacle of getting a bike. With the help of the woman he loves, the hero will get the bike and the job. And, so it would follow, he will get overtime, be promoted to manager, and become president of the company. His marriage will be revived and his heretofore disdainful son will now love and respect him.

Yet, even as the film is packing the formula into the first twenty-three minutes, it is also intruding on its classical patterns and devices, distorting its structure, and preparing for its ultimate dismantling in the climax of the poster-hanging sequence. The opening sequences of the movie establish the use that DeSica will make of narrative structure, characterization, camera work, and music to disengage his film from the conceits and conventions of the Hollywood product. In the opening scene, for example, it takes the camera a while to locate the hero. He is not on the bus that pulls into the piazza; neither has he joined the throng of unemployed who race to and push up the steps of the government's employment office. The functionary who assigns the jobs calls out Ricci's name, but the camera must wait until his friend leads it to him.

Immediately under revision in the action of the scene is the causality-based continuity of American film. Introduced in its place is the structure, theme and style of chance. The randomness of the lottery through which Ricci gets the job is paralleled by the almost casual introduction of him to the audience. Likewise, even when identified, the character does not seem like a hero; he is not star quality but average in looks and devoid of any hint of charisma. In short, while the plot is anxious to get underway, both the dawdling camera and the recumbent protagonist retard the action. Even in its title, the film provides a caution against jumping to facile narrativizing about how the hero's economic and domestic problems will be solved. While the job-giver sets in motion the hero's getting the bike, the title is predicting that some bike will be stolen (Scholes, 283). While Ricci learns that he must find the bike, the title directs attention to the thieves who will take it. The impulse of the plot is further retarded by the unCapraesque crowd on the steps who, rather than applauding the hero, want to take his job. Through their complaints, the economy of the Hollywood film's displacement tactics is unmasked. Solving Ricci's problem will in no way relieve the anxieties of the men clustered around him nor does his getting a job seem to inspire any hope that anyone of them will be next. Underscoring these intrusions into classical cause and effect expectations and fostering an alienation from the formula is the haunting and plaintive music that suggests complications outside the plot even as the action seems to plunge forward to the resolution.

The tension of structures found in this opening sequence is repeated and varied throughout the first movement of the film from job-getting to bicycle theft. In these opening moments, the film has juxtaposed to the classical narration an ambiguous view of the events and now will introduce a discourse centered on a non-star hero and open to uncaused and arbitrary facts and events. Even as the Ricci and his wife, Maria, are overcoming the lack-of-bike obstacle, the narration insists on intruding on the plot. Once home, Ricci ponders his fate, while on the wall behind him the pictures of his parents seems to haunt his aspirations, the past somehow impinging its domestic calm on his present anxiety.

More disruptive of the plot pattern is *Bicycle Thieves'* exploitation of one of classical film's favorite narrative conceits: metonymy, the one standing for the many. While Hollywood films insist that the part stands for the whole, DeSica's movie counters that naivete by insisting that the part is no more than a part. In the scene at the government-run hock shop, Maria has gotten the 7,500 lire for the sheets from her trousseau and leaves the counter to reclaim the bike. The camera lingers. It focuses on an elderly, rather emaciated man reluctantly trading in his binoculars, perhaps surrendering his last pleasure of bird-watching. Here the film has set aside Ricci's predicament to suggest yet another story of human deprivation amidst the general misery. Then, as Ricci waits for the clerk to return his bike, the camera follows his gaze and slowly booms up over thousands and thousands of sheets, hinting at an equal number of family crises and plights beyond the plot of the film. These images dispel the notion that in resolving the crises of one family, it is bringing to happy closure the trials facing an entire population. The nightmare of the post-war depression is allowed to stand even as the plot is rushing toward the fantasy of the dream ending associated with classical films.

In addition to fragmenting the plot by alluding to these other narratives, the film insists on reminding the audience that the hero's quick re-possession of the bike, his obtaining of the job, and his reconciliation with his wife and family are all subject to chance. Later, the camera follows Ricci into the work office. There he is surrounded by posters of the classical films. Even as his co-worker urges him to set down the bicycle and not to be afraid of losing it, the title is still working against the tide of the plot's facile resolving of Ricci's problems. Visually, the positioning of the bike in the foreground in the following scene at the Seer's house sustains the film's ambiguity. Like the job, the thieves could arrive at any moment, and here the bike left on the street seems an open invitation for them. With a craft every bit as manipulative as Hollywood's, this film's randomness attacks the lack of realism in the classical, enclosed, cause and effect structure. Even as its plot is following the classical structure and seeming to endorse those same standardized themes and myths that support the dominant capitalist ideology of the film industry, *Bicycle Thieves* is through camera, mise-en-scène, and symbol roughing up the structure and equating the classical film with romantic illusion and deceit.

Though his goal achievement depends on both the luck of the draw and on his wife's initiative, Ricci is, through the bike, restored to his romantic lead and to his role as master of the house. Referring to Maria's visit to the Seer's as nonsense, he calls her "dumb, dumb," then puts her on the crossbar of the bike and peddles on home. (Later in the film, Ricci out of desperation will return to the nonsense by going to the Seer's.) For this romantic interlude, the film employs a folksy kind of music at odds with the sadder major musical theme that dominates the film. This scene constitutes the apex of Andy Hardy-style family happiness toward which the plot aspires. The crises resolutions continue to accumulate as once inside the house, the now employed and empowered father becomes the idol of his son, Bruno. Made independent by his own employment at a gas station, the son even here maintains some of the critical views he had of his jobless father, but now Bruno's habitual looking up to the father, his imitating of the man's gestures, and (through care for his baby sister) his showing paternal instincts of his own reveal how deeply he has longed for this moment when the father is the provider and wise ruler.

In the manner of the classical Hollywood film, the plot has displaced onto Ricci the burdens of the socioeconomic systems of Italy and resolved them through the melodrama about the bicycle. The ease with which the plot has settled the employment problem and reconciled the family, however, is challenged here by the film's symbolism, specifically through the foregrounding of the dent in the bicycle which acts dialectically in the frame to qualify Bruno's admiration for his father. "What the dent reveals, then, is the vast difference between a film aesthetic which privileges consideration of plot and one in which metaphoric meanings are given equal dignity and weight" (Marcus, 60). There is a triple kind of abrasiveness in the scratch. First, it impedes the forward thrust of the plot toward happy closure; the family world is no longer perfect. Secondly, allied with the title, the dent hints of another action to follow that is not circumscribed by the formula being followed thus far. Thirdly, the dent also locates the son's reluctance to accept the father as omnipotent figurehead; Ricci is no Judge Hardy. The dent circumscribes the otherwise total admiration of the boy for the father as paternal and foreshadows the new kind of relationship that will have to be established after the bike is gone. This latter view is encouraged here through the repetition of the plaintive melody counterpointed with the dominant romantic folksy tune.

In the next sequence, the film's style and imagery continue to affirm the romantic ending of the melodrama. After playfully tussling with Maria and now with his son riding on the bike with him, Ricci sets off to work. Here a new triumphal melody swells behind the action of the bike's gliding through the streets of Rome. The scenes are thoroughly inscribed by the plot resolutions; yet after twenty minutes, the implications of the title still hang over the action. Stalemated between ending and beginning, the sequence further unmasks the conventions of the classical film. The ease with which success has found Ricci and re-solved his economic and family problems implies the kind of naivete on the part of the audience that would find this kind of movie entertaining or related in any way to their lives. DeSica's film is then criticizing producers, films, and audience. The film mocks the notion of the sim-ple-minded kind of ploy by the brevity with which the action brings the hero to triumphal victories over poverty and domestic discontent. Ricci here recalls the taxi driver who became the radio star then the opera singer. The action puts the hero on such a positive roll and with such momentum that only a few sequences would seem to stand between him as poster hanger and him as movie mogul. This implication of sim-ple-minded, fantastic, and irrelevant plots and standardized themes in movies becomes more explicit as the film begins to employ its most graphic use of intertextual imagery.

The closing action of the Hollywood plot in *Bicycle Thieves* in-volves Ricci's pasting up the poster of Rita Hayworth. Prior to that mundane business, he must first learn how to put up the poster. During that lesson even the camera seems to weary of the success-finds-Ricci scenario; it seems anxious to get onto more engaging content. As the scene opens, the interest is quickly divided between the instructions to Ricci and the begging of the little kids playing the accordion. Initially and literally, the kids are kicked aside by Ricci's co-worker and told to beat it. The camera, however, pans and follows the kids as they pursue a bourgeois gentleman who walks on and ignores their begging. The camera choice does not start another plot or story; rather, it establishes the theme of investigating a society's moral condition by examining its treatment of children. That use of victimized children, familiar to DeSica's earlier films, will be picked up in *Bicycle Thieves'* showing the neglect and abuse that befalls Ricci's son, Bruno (Liehm, 49). In this scene, the film privileges this theme and subordinates the plot ac-tion of the classical film. The focus is further divided by the privileging of the dialogue from the plot over the unrelated image of the children begging. Referring to their job, the co-worker advises Ricci: "You must have the eye and be quick." The phrase seems doubly ironic. Visually those words are joined to the image of the bourgeois man who refuses to see those most in need. Very shortly, Ricci, because he is neither watchful nor quick, will join the children in being abused then ignored by the society around him. In ignoring the lesson about poster hanging, the camera anticipates the dismissal of the whole Hollywood plot, literally just around the corner, and the replacement of it with the thematic investigation of the city. The scene connects man and child to the indifference of society and prepares the spectator for the transitional action ahead that will re-introduce and expand on those themes (Bondanella, 59).

The framing in the poster scene does not bridge a gap between the classical film and the one DeSica is making. Rather, it recapitulates the history of the neorealistic film movement as it divorced itself from then returned to the primacy of commercial requisites in the cinema system. The framing of the action pulls the viewer's attention away from Hollywood and into Rome. Now overtly, the film exploits intertextual film imagery to begin a new cycle (Bondanella, 6). In a film marked, as Tomasulo and Marcus have noted, by periodic references to film, this section of *Bicycle Thieves* opens with a disruption of the male gaze, made even more explicitly intertextual by the choice of subject: Rita Hayworth, Hollywood's leading femme fatale poster-woman of the Forties. As the spectator beholds her face, Ricci's hands reach into the frame; the intervention reminding us that we are looking at a film and that we are not Ricci. As the camera pulls back, it reveals his own amorous posture: the spread of his open arms matching those of the alluring Rita Hayworth in the poster. At the same time, the new point of view of a long shot ventilates the closed Hollywood world by establishing the real city context around the poster. The images symbolize several contrasts at work in the scene: Hayworth vs. Ricci, American wealth vs. Italian poverty, and melodramatic fantasy vs. the quotidian in the real world, to mention a few. The film, then, may identify with Ricci in an ironic way that understands his infatuation with Hollywood and with the plot in which he is involved and at the same time, through the intrusiveness of these movie images, the movie adopts a different, more omniscient perspective, one less respectful of those conventions that have ensnared the hero. Through the temporality and spaciality of the shot which gradually opens out to reveal the whole world, the film strikes a new stance toward the poster, toward Ricci, toward the environment, and toward the earlier plot. Nick Browne has described this use of time and space strategy: "the presentational structures which shape the action both convey a point of view and define the course of reading, and are fundamental to the exposition of moral ideas...." (117). What the film's dual perspective encourages is an aesthetic-moral attitude. Specifically, Ricci, like the old film noir victim, can be seen as a "sucker for a dame" and for the system that fashioned that image and for the fantastic ideology on which it depends. What he is drawn to, however, the film disdains.

At this juncture of the film, Ricci's vision is redirected away from the poster, away from the fantasy, and, eventually, away from the bike. He is not, after all, Cary Grant. Likewise, the film is determining its audience on the basis of this education of vision. The old audience, perhaps including those women of Naples, who swallowed the Hollywood-American myth of hard work and a little luck overcoming all the social problems can now leave (stomp out of) the theater. As the imminent theft of the bike establishes, there is an everyday reality that defies tidy structure and solutions. To the poster's image of ersatz sex, luxury, and danger, the film now juxtaposes the well-rehearsed theater of the streets as its three principals enter the frame. While Ricci devotes himself to Hollywood's image, the antagonists (perhaps former owners of the sheets at the hock shop) take up their positions for this new show. Each of the three thieves studies his part and waits for his cue. Thief, blocker, and misdirector, even the taxi driver, introduce to the film the ordinary, accidental problems that withstand the quick-fix plot solutions favored

121

by classical film. The film of the title is now ready to replace the classical Hollywood movie seen thus far. The editing of the scene with the quick cuts from the theft of the bike to Ricci's alarm, to the chase and to the complete disappearance of the thief in less than a minute depict a Ricci shocked out of the lethargy that has characterized his point of view and his actions. He has missed the warning signs of workers who would take his job, of the dented bicycle, and of the children begging in the streets. In this capricious world, he is no star, no almighty provider, and no wise man. Like his paternalism, Ricci's other Hollywood-fed hopes are dashed by the arbitrary choice of his bike as target and by the capricious, inexplicable disappearance of it and the thieves.

When the bikeless hero returns to the poster, his education continues. First he must close the chapter of the Hollywood film. His disenchantment is turned on the poster which he tries to ignore by tossing aside his brush and then reluctantly smacks down with a few strokes. The camera now refocuses the film by panning away from the poster and by privileging a shot that tracks in on the face of the hero. "The opulent glamour of Rita Hayworth...is set against the grim poverty of Antonio...." (Armes, 152). At this point this unique tracking shot also isolates Ricci from the environment and heightens his alienation from the city and the streets' indifference to him. The tracking here makes explicit the new direction of the film. Momentarily, the movie, like the hero, is brought to a standstill. A neorealist caesura has replaced the Hollywood suture of the sequences. The film must begin again.

Bicycle Thieves' use the film imagery endorses a new anti-white telephone, anti-Hollywood, anti-studio system kind of movie, one which is closer in style and structure to the less plotted films. As Aristarco observes, "...*Potemkin*,... *Tabu*. ...*The Kid*, ...*Man of Iran*: these are among the few works most exalted in the history of the art. "Art" and "plot" are two terms in continual separation" (Aristarco, 5). What replaces the plot is virtually a cinema of chance that suggests the cruelties of the socioeconomic world on the one hand and a fatal view of human experience on the other. "All my films," DeSica said," are about the search for human solidarity. In *The Bicycle Thieves,* the solidarity occurs but how long does it last? Twenty-four hours. One experiences only moments of solidarity" (Samuels, 149).

Likewise brief was the attempt by Italian filmmakers to separate themselves from Hollywood. Eventually DeSica too would return to a commercial films. What seems especially appropriate is that one gateway for the return to conventional production would also be punctuated by the gaze on a woman's body and that the shot would describe a shift from realism and a return to Hollywood. almost reversing the use of perspective in the poster scene's final shot, the pivotal shot in *Bitter Rice* (Giuseppe De Santis, 1949) closes out the real world for the glamour world. Describing the scene in which Anna Magnani is pulling up her skirt, Silverman concludes: "Our eyes no longer watch the right side of the frame, the mass of working women, but take in the movement of the skirt, the revelation once again of the body. Not only voyeurism and the gaze, not only the Bazanian middle distances but the documentable trace of American capital investment is marked by the movement of that skirt" (Silverman, 43). That systematic gesture and selection of perspectives can serve as closure on the period of independent Italian filmmaking and as paradoxical reversal of the use of intertextuality by DeSica's *Bicycle Thieves.*

NOTES

[1]Guido Aristarco, *"Ladri di Biciclette." Cinema,* 1.7, (1949).

[2]Roy Armes, *Patterns of Realism.* New York: A.S. Barnes and Company, 1971.

[3]Peter Bondanella, *Italian Cinema.* New York: Frederick Ungar Publishing Co., 1983.

[4]Raymond Borde, quoted by George Huaco in *The Sociology of Film Art,* New York: Basic Books, 1965.

[5]David Bordwell, Janet Staiger, and Kristin Thompson. *The Classical Hollywood Cinema.* New York: Columbia University Press, 1985.

[6]Nick Browne, "The Spectator in the Text: The Rhetoric of Stagecoach." *Narrative, Apparatus, Ideology.* Ed. Philip Rosen. New York: Columbia University Press, 1986.

[7]Nicola Chiaromonte, "Rome Letter." *Partisan Review* June, 1949: 626.

[8]Vittorio DeSica, Interview in Charles Thomas Samuels, *Encountering Directors.* New York: G.P. Putnam's Sons, 1972.

[9]..., "Why *Ladri di Biciclette." Springtime in Italy.* Ed. David Overby. Hamden, CN.: 1978.

[10]Jean Genet, "Letters from Rome." *New Yorker* 12 Mar. 1949: 66 and 7 July 1949: 40.

[11]Foster Hirsch, *The Dark Side of the Screen: Film Noir.* New York: A.S. Barnes and Company, 1981.

[12]George Huaco, *The Sociology of Film Art.* New York: Basic Books, 1965.

[13]Mira Liehm, *Passion and Defiance.* Berkeley, CA.: University of California Press, 1984.

[14]Millicent Marcus, *Italian Film in the Light of Neorealism.* Princeton, NJ.: Princeton University Press, 1986.

[15]David Overby, *Springtime in Italy.* Hamden, CN.: Anchor Books, 1978.

[16]Tino Ranieri, "DeSica neorealista." *Il Neorealismo Cinematografico Italiano, Alti del convegno della X Monstra Internationale del Nuovo Cinema.* Ed. Lino Miccihe. Venice: Marsilio Editore, 1975.

[17]Argeo Santucci, *Motion Picture and Television Almanac 1953-1954.* in George Huaco. *The Sociology of Film Art.* New York: Basic Books, 1965.

[18]Robert Scholes, "Narration and Narrativity in Film," *Quarterly Review of Film Studies,* 1.3., August 1976.

[19]Michael Silverman, "Italian Film and American Capital 1947-1951." *Cinema Histories, Cinema Practices.* Eds. Patricia Mellencamp and Philip Rosen. Frederick, Md.: University Publications of America, 1984.]

[20]Frank Tomasulo, "The Bicycle Thieves: A Re-Reading." *Cinema Journal* 21.2, Spring 1982.

10. PICTURES OF PICTURES: REFERENCE AND REALITY IN TWO SCRIPT VERSIONS OF *POTEMKIN*

Bruce E. Fleming

THE OBSERVATION WITH WHICH I BEGIN is a perceptual one thus a perception that is necessarily my own, but one which I believe to be more general as well. Namely, that the printed script of a film produces in the reader a greater sense of what we may call "realism" than do other printed works, such as novels or plays—so that we might almost say it exists in a relation of signification to its object closer than the description of most other literary objects. I will be basing my consideration of this phenomenon here on two printed scenarios of Eisenstein's *Potemkin*: the version edited by Jay Leyda from Eisenstein's shooting script and that prepared by David Meyer from the print of the finished film at New York's Museum of Modern Art. (The latter kind of script is what Leyda, in the introduction to his volume, calls a shot-list.)

Once we have accepted that film scripts do produce such a sense of realism (and I will be giving examples from these scripts to exemplify the phenomenon) we may then go on to ask why they do so. I propose that this effect is produced by the fact of the script's double reference: film scripts are pictures of pictures in two media simultaneously, being written pictures of visual ones. On a primary level the script refers to the film of which it is a printed record; on a secondary level it refers to the content of that film. Yet the reality effect is due as well to the fact that the film script refers, at least in part, to an external referent (namely the film) that is *absent* for the reader of the printed script. This conclusion with respect to the film script allows us to see in addition that the reality effect many theorists have thought to obtain with films themselves is produced under the same circumstances—namely in the case of a binary reference relation where we feel the absence of a substantial referent. From this, finally, we see that this much-discussed reality effect of films is by no means a quality of the medium itself—as is frequently suggested—but is instead the result of a particular configuration of referents whose achievement may be the exception rather than the rule.

The printed film script is thus a rather peculiar object. Yet we find a reference to something like it in Proust's *A la recherche du temps perdu*, where the narrator recalls that his grandmother liked to hang on her walls pictures of famous buildings such as the Cathedral of Chartres or the Chateau of Saint-Cloud, but in the form of photographic reproductions of paintings rather than photographs of the monuments themselves. To an even greater extent, however, she preferred engravings of pictures of the famous monuments—and these, if possible, of the work in a state in which it no longer existed. Her preference, therefore, was for pictures of pictures, as if (the narrator explains) she were thereby inserting into the relationship multiple thicknesses of art, rendering less mechanical the reproduction of reality by the photograph.[2]

The film script is like the pictures of Proust's grandmother in that it too is a picture of a picture, though in two different media. It exists in a relation both to the filmic artifact which is its most immediate object of representation as well as to the outside reality which is the object of this film—so that the relation of the script with the world outside is at once single- and double-layered. And this, I propose, is a fact of perception as well: during our experience of reading, the script seems to refer to

128

(or as I will be saying shortly, to evoke) both the film and that to which the film refers, simultaneously yet separately. It brings this content before us, make it visualizable and visualized to a degree that is rare with other written works.

The scripts from which I draw my examples are the two versions of Eisenstein's *Potemkin* mentioned above. Though my conclusion is that all the different kinds of scripts that exist evoke these two realities at least to some extent and thus for my purposes are more similar than divergent, we reach this conclusion by insisting, at any rate initially, on the divergences between types of scripts. The first thing we notice on comparing these two versions is certainly that they differ as to the amount of detail offered: the Leyda/Eisenstein shooting script gives brief indications of what is happening; the Mayer shot-list breaks the action down into many individual happenings. This difference, film scholars would point out, is a result of the fact that we are dealing with different kinds of objects, one of which reproduces a state of the film "before," the other "after." Not all film scripts are alike, and not all exist in exactly the same degree of relation to what we may call their two realities. Why, we may wonder, should we try to compare these two at all? The answer to this question is that they are both literary objects, written works that can be read and reacted to—leaving out of consideration the explanation of their genesis or purpose with respect to the film

From the point of view of the filmmaker and the historian of that process, of course, this aspect is precisely the one that matters. It is, I acknowledge, a literary point of view that conceives of film scripts as being more alike than different. For the case can be made rather easily that film scripts should be considered as a unified genre (or perhaps sub-genre) in the standard division of literary works into novel, poetry, drama, essay, and short story, given that most scripts possess qualities both of the play and of the novel. What sets them off from the other genres, of course, is precisely this fact of their primary reference to yet another art object outside of themselves. And it is this that gives them their peculiar capacity to produce an effect of "realism."

At any rate I acknowledge freely that it is only in perception after the fact, by a reader, that all scripts can be considered as if of the same sort. Yet I do not expect such a point of departure as this to raise many eyebrows in a literary theoretical climate such as ours influenced by the reader-reception theory of the School of Constance (whose most well-known names are those of Jauss and Iser) and by Deriddean deconstruction, which resolutely considers all written artifacts as "texts" of equal intrinsic importance. Logically enough, at any rate, it is a claim related to an effect on the reader that is central to my consideration here—namely, that the film script somehow exists in a closer relation of representation to both of its two levels of signification that would, say, a novel based on the film (itself a hot contemporary genre, thanks to the pressures of the market).

Let us then consider both the differences and ultimate similarities between these two script versions of *Potemkin*, starting with this fact of what seems greater detail in Mayer's version. In the episode where the cook cuts up the maggoty meat prior to putting it in the soup, for example, the Eisenstein/Leyda shooting script renders the action as two separate shots that read only as follows: "Ship's cooks hack up the meat. Meat being chopped" (Leyda p.16). The Mayer script, working from one print of the finished product, has eight shots, and the page including them reads as follows (p.50):

> The cook enters with the joint of meat, closes the door, picks up the axe and lays the meat on the chopping block
>
> *(Cut to . . .)*
> The cook raises the axe above his head, brings it swiftly down and raises it again.
>
> *(Cut to . . .)*
> The cook raises his axe, hacks at the joint of meat, then turns to comment to another cook behind him. He again raises the axe as sailors rush into the galley to plead with him to stop preparing the meat.

(Cut to . . .)
As the cook lifts the axe over his head and chops downward
with the blade, two sailors crowd close behind him

(Cut to . . .)
The axe-head strikes the tough meat on the chopping block
without splitting it. The axe raises out of the frame, then de-
scends swiftly, barely denting the joint.

(Cut to . . .)
As the cook swings the axe downward, the two sailors pull
at his arms to interfere with his work.

(Cut to . . .)
The cook yanks the joint off the chopping block and swings
it angrily away from the two sailors. He puts the meat back
on the block, raises his axe, then puts it down again.

(Cut to . . .)
The joint of meat on the block fills the screen. A sailor's
hand points at rotted areas of the meat. It is withdrawn as
the axe-head strikes the joint without cutting it..

And the margins here give both numbers and indications for placing
these shots in the continuity of the film, as well as a classification of the
shot with respect to camera distance.

I must assume for the sake of my argument that this example has
made evident the capacity of the script to make us "see" the content of
the film, at least in the Mayer version. Yet if this is so the reason it is
so, I think, is not because of Mayer's precision with respect to the content of the film. It is, rather, because this detailed text makes us conscious of references to aspects which are not those of the content of the
film at all, the references to the frame ("the axe rises out of the frame",
"the joint of meat on the block fills the screen") and the repetition of the
word "cut" which underlines both the composition of the individual
frame, and the montage.

This effect seems strongest at those points in the Mayer script when words are used that avoid the whole-body or independent individual designations of the traditional novel—that tell us that we *see* rather than what is "going on." One particularly successful example of this, I think, is the episode of the dishwasher, which does not appear in the Eisenstein/Leyda shooting script at all (pp. 62-63).

> A hand places freshly dried soup spoons face downward on a cloth near a teapot.
>
> *(Cut to ...)*
>
> The arm of the sailor washing dishes in the pail is seen from behind as he gives washed plates to another for drying.
>
> *(Cut to ...)*
>
> *(From above)* The dishwasher hands a plate to a sailor and wipes his nose with the back of his wet wrist. He is the sailor who was lashed by the boatswain while sleeping below deck.
>
> *(Cut to ...)*
>
> Two more freshly dried soup spoons are placed face downwards on the cloth.
>
> *(Cut to ...)*
>
> The intent face of one of the two sailors drying the dishes fills the screen. His lips are pursed, his brows down as he concentrates on his work.
>
> *(Cut to ...)*
>
> The dishwasher's arm, seen from behind, hands another dish to a dryer.
>
> *(Cut to ...)*
>
> The brows of the sailor drying dishes are drawn. His cheeks puff from his exertions.
>
> *(Cut to ...)*

(*From above*) Two hands scrub the bottom of a large dark plate being held over the washing pail.

Yet the effect of a vivid perception of all these hands and plates will be reduced if the description of this shot is at all "flowery," so that we become more conscious of the words before us. This is undeniably the case in the Mayer shot-list, so that the Eisenstein/Leyda version, despite its paucity of detail, seems in contrast to possess a certain power to evoke the content of the film that almost makes up for its lack of subdivisions or virtually any references to the qualities of the celluloid. For example, the first scene in the shooting script is given simply as "Iris in. Waves breaking." (Leyda p. 15). We contrast this simple yet somehow powerful evocation of waves breaking by merely saying they are (much as Hemingway says that water is cold by merely telling us it is) to what seems the over-elaborate prose of Mayer's version, of which I give only the first three shots (p. 33):

A wave hurls itself against a stubborn, craggy breakwater jutting across a harbor.

(Cut to . . .)
The powerful waves tumble forward over the rocks, seeking a weak point at the breakwater's base.

(Cut to . . .)
The ceaseless probing continues as another wave breaks over the low jetty.

One would like to re-write these to eliminate most of the adjectives, and to neutralize the verbs. In fact, the Eisenstein script, as I suggest, gets its evocative power precisely from this neutrality of vocabulary. I quote a short series of shot directions for consideration, also from the sequences showing the preparation of the soup (p. 17):

The meat being thrown into the cauldron.
The meat being hacked.
The cauldron bubbling.

(Dissolve to seething faces of the sailors)
Signal for the meal
An officer goes into the men's mess.
Empty tables.
The officer looks [at the empty tables].
Untouched bowls.

But why should words like *cut, frame*, and *dissolve*—which refer only to the film and are overtly words of meta-reference—have this power to make us see not only the film to which they refer, but also the content of that film? Why should a writing style that makes us conscious of the written object as possessing qualities in itself not identical to those of the film to which it refers detract from this "reality effect"? The explanation has to do, I suggest, with binary contrast, and with the fact that the first level of this contrast is overtly not before us. For it seems that the power of the film script to evoke the world of the film is the most intense when the printed object makes clearest the contrast between form and content in this absent film, and when the style in which this content (which thus refers to an external world) is given is the most bland, the least "literary"—which prevents our being two conscious of yet a third layer, that of the printed object itself. (Proust's grandmother, it seems, would not have approved of my conclusion here.)

Nonetheless, this power is extant to some extent in all film scripts—it suffices for us to know (rather than being constantly re malned of this fact, as a script like Mayer's does) that the script refers to an extant, though manifestly un-present film in order to make this quality of immediacy of content appear. The inclusion of the certain number of still shots from the film, moreover, encourages this effect with all published scripts. For this tends to convince us emotionally that the film, in fact, does exist somewhere—as well as giving us hints on how to visualize the words. Having seen, for example, Isabelle Adjani dressed as Adele H. in one single still shot, we know the basic characteristics of her height, face, and costumes, and can apply these to many of the divergent situations in the scenario.

Film scripts may therefore be arranged along a continuum, one that these two versions of *Potemkin* help us plot. We have only to extend them outwards in two directions towards, at one extreme, a book full of chronologically ordered still shots from the film—a kind of printed viewer's digest of the celluloid that is hardly literary at all, and in the other direction, towards a kind of film script that reads like an amalgam of a novel and a play and fits very securely between these genres. The scripts most capable of evoking the sense of "realism" to which I am referring fall somewhere in the middle.

There are many examples of the first, including the *Bibliothèque des Classiques du Cinéma* published by Balland in Paris. Most of Ingmar Bergman's film scripts are of the second sort—unsurprisingly, since they are written before the film is made, and are not yet even shooting scripts. All of them contain details that the film cannot convey—the script of *The Serpent's Egg*, for example, tells us what Liv Ullmann's cabaret smells of (urine); sensations of the characters are frequently expressed in a form that cannot be so indicated in the image. The last sentence of *Smiles of a Summer Night*, for example, goes as follows: "Frid walks behind her, and the sight of her rounded thighs is so damn beautiful that he begins to sing."[3]

Yet I believe that it is not this Bergmanesque kind of script, with its reduction of two levels of signification to one, which evokes most intensely the world portrayed in the film. The experience of reality in the film script seems, paradoxically enough, most intense precisely in those scripts which acknowledge that they are scripts of *films* rather than attempting to pass as descriptions of external reality in unmediated form: scripts that do not try to short-cut the touch to the world outside by obliterating references to the film that stands between them. This usually means those scripts that give the maximum of technical detail from the film regarding the type of shot (close up to long shot or dolly shot), use the special masking techniques such as the iris, and precise nature of each continuity (dissolve, wipe, fade-out, and so on). In addition, the nature of the literary style and content within the shots also plays a role. In short, they evoke in most detail the object to which the script refers, but which is absent from it: the film, rather than the content of the film. All scripts, therefore, evoke their absent referent to some extent, but some do so more intensely than others.

My conclusion is thus that it is the contrast between the two levels of signification in a film script (the film, and the world of the film) that produces this "reality effect" with scripts—and that the clearer the contrast is, the greater the effect will be. Our reality effect, it seems, is strongest when we have one layer that (so to say) takes on itself the burden of the signification, leaving free the other layer to seem pure signified—even though this is something that we know it cannot, in fact, be. Both, of course, are expressed in the medium of print—and the contrast only seems so absolute because the commonality of the medium of print is not foregrounded. A florid style of writing, however, makes us too conscious of this layer, this medium—and so lessens what otherwise seems the so satisfyingly absolute break between the two levels *its* signification.

Yet this binary relation is produced so clearly because we are dealing with a first level that is absent: at each moment in reading the film script we are conscious that it is the script of *something,* and more precisely something that we do not have. In a sense, the effect of reality in film scripts is produced because we "desire" the film (to use a term much in vogue in Lacanian literary analysis), which is to say, we have it held so tantalizingly before us as unattainable.

All this makes clear that it cannot be the medium of film itself which is producing the reality effect. Indeed, my consideration of the realism of printed film scripts has already made it seem improbable that the filmic medium would be the deciding factor: if it were an effect of the medium, how can it be that printed scripts produce it so strongly? The importance of the implications of this conclusion for film theory in general seems, in fact, of the first order. Specifically, it is clear that an assumption regarding medium is at the basis of all of the theories which involve the notion that film (and its related medium, photography) somehow reproduce the world more closely than, say, painting. (These theories include both of what are usually taken to be the two major competing schools of film theory, those associated with Bazin and Kracauer on the one hand and with Eisenstein and Arnheim on the other—as well as neo-Marxist thinkers such as Benjamin, structuralists such as Roland Barthes, and all-arounds such as Susan Sontag.) Yet I do not think that film itself possesses this capacity.

Roman Jakobson, writing in 1921, suggested that "realism" was an effect rather than an absolute quality. He proposed not only that one man's reality is another man's artificiality, but that reality is an effect that could only be achieved by constantly altering the techniques used for producing it: since the reality of one generation becomes the artificiality of the subsequent generation.[4] Such relational theses were, of course, standard for the Russian (and later Prague). Formalists, as was the particular historicist form this argument takes here. It is my suggestion as well that "realism" is a relational effect, though it is not necessarily one of contrast to preceding works. It is instead the result of the specific kind of binary reference relation involving an absent, substantial referent.

In the early years of cinema, for example, it was common to assert a form of this belief in the realism of the filmic medium itself (the fear of the audiences who watched Lumière's train pull into the station is widely cited). Yet this sense, I suggest, was the result of just such a contrast as I am claiming to be necessary here for the perception of "reality in a film script. Film seemed realistic, that is, first of all by contrast with painting, or with theatre (a contention with which the Formalists would agree)—but this was so only because the contrast made the referent seem substantial. In order to produce this sense of realism, however, it was necessary for this substantialized and somehow foregrounded referent to be *absent* as well. It was not, that is, because the spectators recognized the image of a train that they found the film "realistic," but rather because they were surprised at not being run over by this image.

Thus when we speak of the sensation of realism in film, or film scripts, it is not because of some inherent relation between the medium used in reference and that to which it refers. Instead, this sensation is produced when we are acutely conscious both of a substantial, independent referent, and of the absence of this referent—as the film for the film script is substantial, yet absent. Another example of this is our entranced state before the photographs of Atget—precisely because the world they portray is separated from us by time and destruction: the image which would otherwise float on its reference like a contact lens on an eye has suddenly been bereft of its support, and so takes on the strange quality of seeming to stand in for this entire manifold, takes over its ontic status. (The only reason Atget could take such photographs is because he himself sensed that the world they portrayed was disappearing.) The realism we sometimes sense with films and photographs is not an effect of the medium alone, but of a certain set of circumstances: our snapshots of now-dead Aunt Sally seem to call up the past by its hair, but the Polaroid of our picnic newly issued from the camera is merely amusing.

By the same token the photographs in *National Geographic* seem "real" because the sub-cultures they portray are both part of our world, and far away. (We must believe that someone has *gone somewhere* and taken these: if they were taken in a studio in California they suddenly do not seem real, though their content is the same.) And a photograph of the U.S. Capitol does not, for the man who cleans it, produce this mesmerized devouring the image that we associate with the sensation of realism—precisely because the referent is so available, and so quotidian. (This is the reason we do not think fashion photographs more "realistic" than fashion drawings, or see the 3-D pencil drawings of empty clothes that Banana Republic has adopted for its catalogue as more realistic than the standard newspaper clothes ad of stylized hatching: the purpose of an ad is to give us information, not to evoke a manifold of information we already have.) The reason a Renoir film seems "realistic," is partly because of the contrast to an Eisenstein or a

138

Vertov, so that we are made aware of the long shots and outdoor scenes—but ultimately because these, in turn, evoke for us a world portrayed that, we see, is *not in the movie theater*. And the reason we may think *Ivan the Terrible* "unrealistic" is not because it lacks such scenes, but rather because the world portrayed is not independently a part of our ken in any way: we do not sense any binary contrast, and the images are identical with their referent.

In order for this sensation of realism to be produced, then, we must first of all be dealing with two layers of reference. Furthermore, the primary level of reference must be both substantial, and absent. If either of these last two conditions is not fulfilled (the first in *Ivan the Terrible*, the second for the man who cleans the Capitol) the photographic or filmic image does not produce its effect of realism. "Realism" is not a general quality of the photographic/filmic medium—but rather a fact of particular circumstances that may be limited to the situation of a single perceiver.

NOTES

[1]David Mayer, *Eisenstein's Potemkin: A shot by shot presentation* (New York: Grossman, 1972). Jay Leyda, ed., *Eisenstein: Three Films* (New York: Harper and Row, 1974).

[2]Marcel Proust, *A la recherche du temps perdu* (Paris: Gallimard, 1954), vol. 1, p.40.

[3]*Four Screenplays of Ingmar Bergman* (New York: Simon and Schuster). Here, p. 94.

[4]Ladislav Matejka and Krystyna Pomorska, *Readings in Russian Poetics: Formalist and Structuralist Views.* (Cambridge, Mass.: MIT Press, 1971). pp. 38-46.

11. THE COMPOUND GENRE FILM: *BILLY THE KID VERSUS DRACULA* MEETS *THE HARVEY GIRLS*

Adam Knee

ALTHOUGH IT IS COMMONPLACE to note the proliferation of varied genre combinations in commercial films of the eighties, the notion of what precisely, constitutes and characterizes a compound genre film has been very little discussed. My aim in this essay will be to expand on the notion of the compound genre film through an examination of a number of texts whose generic interactions are perhaps somewhat plainer and clearer than the generic pyrotechnics of many films now in the market place. I will shy from the term "genre hybrid" here because these films are not organically-derived entities in which two or more sets of generic conventions have somehow become one (in which case we, indeed, would not even be able to perceive the text as having a compound nature); these films develop not as a result of natural evolutionary forces acting upon supposed "elemental" genres, but are rather functions of numerous social and historical determinants and can come into being by any number of routes. What foremost characterizes a compound genre film for us is that it concurrently engages multiple distinct and relatively autonomous horizons of generic expectation; the extent to which these horizons remain distinct is the extent to which we perceive the text as being compound in its generic nature.[1]

If a genre has over time developed certain characteristics which happen to coincide with those of another genre, we do not perceive it as moving into the realm of the compound genre; the shared elements do not seem alien, but rather constitute accepted conventions. Thus, we do not experience the singing cowboy film (e.g., a Gene Autry film) as a compound genre so much as part of a western sub-genre, stemming from traditions of singing cowboy performers and of song-singing interludes existing even in silent westerns. The western musical (e.g., *Seven Brides for Seven Brothers* [1954]), on the other hand, calls forth multiple sets of expectations—the western's characters, locales, and situations, for example, employed concurrently with the musical's formal techniques and narrative patterns. At the same time, however, the western musical has itself become familiar to us over time, has developed its own horizon of expectations, and to this extent it, like any other generic combination, loses some of its compound nature with repetition, becomes a distinct genre in and of itself. Indeed, to the extent that, as Jauss has argued, no text can be perceived without a "specific situation of understanding" (79), without its own distinct horizon of expectations, there is no such thing as a pure compound genre film; what I am discussing here are genre texts which are to varying degrees compound in nature.

Perhaps the most important corollary of multiple generic affinities is an inescapable level of self-consciousness; when two or more sets of generic expectations are thrust together, each one immediately becomes a marked element, and a new level of discourse is of necessity opened up. While this more clearly true for a campy genre send-up like *The Rocky Horror Picture Show* (1975), it is unavoidably also true for compound genre films more in keeping with the conventions of classical Hollywood narrative, such as MGM's *The Harvey Girls* (1945), which for the most part attempts to disguise the gaps between its two genres, to achieve a semblance of narrative coherency. To borrow Bakhtin's

142

terminology here, the Hollywood film tends to try to resolve its differing generic "voices," to achieve a higher degree of what we could indeed call "hybridization;"[2] it is at points when such hybridization is unsuccessful, however, that the film's compound nature is most evident.

I do hope the reader will indulge me if I start with what might seem a somewhat crude example to illustrate and elaborate on some of these points; as justification, I will merely note that, as Northrop Frye has pointed out, it is often in the most popular and conventionalized of texts that generic characteristics are most readily observed (104). The title of the text I would first like to discuss, *Billy the Kid versus Dracula* (1966), does indeed, in a sense, tell all: two quite distinct sets of generic conventions have been pulled together and forced into a showdown, a fact which the title immediately and self-consciously draws attention to. The opening minutes of the film quickly reinforce a sense of a playfully heightened generic self-awareness: a campy credit sequence featuring Dracula's name dripping with blood and a kind of bat wipe for changes of titles is followed by an extended, pointed paraphrase of a number of scenes from John Ford's *Stagecoach* (1939). The film's cast in fact includes a featured player from the Ford western, John Carradine, as well as a number of other western film veterans—Olive Carey, Harry Carey Jr., and Roy Barcroft. Carradine's performance as Dracula here, which features ludicrous snarls and bug-eyed stares, is at once overblown and removed, as though he were placing his actions in quotes, exaggeratedly repeating the motions of his previous Dracula roles and thus mocking the generic image with which he has become strongly associated.

There appears to be a level of self-consciousness as well in the film's unusually low production values and excessively clumsy formal technique, characteristics which a low budget does not necessarily force on a film. The film's shoddiness seems all the more striking when one considers that the director, William Beaudine, had to have gained at least some technical competence during a prolific directorial career extending back to 1914 (albeit primarily at poverty row studios from the

'40s on). *Billy the Kid versus Dracula* removes the illusion from its il-lusions, makes its own transparency visible. Sets and props are of such poor quality they seem to broadcast their own artifice, and many scenes offer a very narrow, claustrophobic visual coverage of setting, presum-ably in order to obviate extensive set construction. A saloon interior is a plain wood-panelled room with a few tables, the walls covered with Indian rugs in a gesture toward authenticity. Dime store plastic flowers serve as the requisite wolfs-bane, and a sickly looking rubber bat seems to have come from a similar source. Dracula's materializations and de-materializations, as well as transformations involving the bat, are them-selves pointedly clumsy and even disorienting.

At times the film's formal "cheapness" works in tandem with Carradine's campy performance style, underscoring its very overstated-ness. Each time he starts to hypnotize a young woman, for example, his eyes bulging, a red light is suddenly, crassly cast upon his face; in one such instance he first stares at the camera (which clearly suggests that the shot is from the victim's perspective), then bends forward and out of the frame to bite the victim's neck (which clearly suggests the shot is not from the victim's perspective). By means of both performance style and formal technique, then, generic gestures are worked to death and stripped of any real expressive function, character motivations both laid bare and relieved of any inherent dramatic import; all seem subjugated to one broad generic joke. In a sense, the film is not about its characters and setting, etc., but about generic conventions themselves—and specifically, given the film's flaunting of its low budget, about B-genre conventions, about the type of filmmaking Beaudine had been involved with for decades.

This is by no means an attempt to argue that *Billy the Kid versus Dracula* constitutes any kind of radical filmmaking praxis. While the film does have a strong degree of reflexivity and mocks aspects of tra-ditional Hollywood filmmaking, its brazen compoundedness seems far more an inexpensive way of attracting an audience than an oppositional strategy. The text provides an entertainment which, for the most part, is

144

not that far from the norms of more conventional genre films, despite the presence of two distinct generic frameworks, each with its own narrative assumptions. The inescapable differences between the two genres are regulated, and the text endowed with a strong degree of logical coherence, largely through a kind of process of condensation, whereby elements common to both genres, points of intersection between the two sets of conventions, receive heavy emphasis. A key site of such condensation is the film's lead player, Carradine, being an iconographic figure for both the horror and western genres, having played both numerous poverty-row vampires and numerous western character roles; his introduction in the film has him clearly marked as a vampire, but, again, it involves a quotation of scenes from a western he was featured in. His nineteenth-century costume, the horse-drawn carriages he often travels in, and the cave-turned-silver mine he sleeps in all seem appropriate to both the western and the horror film.

Many key secondary characters also have connections to both genres. The Osters, a German immigrant family, fit in with the convention of old-world immigrants in the western (e.g., Lars Jorgensen in *The Searchers* [1956]) and with one of old-world peasants bearing what turn out to be well-grounded fears and superstitions in the horror film. As in the western, we have a tough, drinking frontier doctor (although in an interesting twist she is a woman, here, played by Carey), and as in the horror film, the doctor figure, largely by virtue of her knowledge of vampirism, is crucial to the destruction of Dracula. The doctor's scalpel, owing to its physical similarity to a wooden stake, also plays into the narrative, being what Billy uses to piece the vampire's heart at the film's conclusion. Indeed, the emphasis on death and violence common to both genres (and making them inherently compatible on a certain level) is retained here as well.

While this process of condensation does help make for a more coherent text—a compound genre film sufficiently within the bounds of mainstream narrative cinematic practice to be economically viable—a fundamental characteristic of the film is, again, the continued autonomy of the genres it utilizes. The film's setting, for example, is for the most part pure western: the American frontier in the late nineteenth century. The film's dramatis personae are heavily weighted toward the western genre as well; indeed, only Dracula is clearly a part of the horror genre and even he (because of casting, costume, etc.) is allowed to enter here into both horror and western discourses. The visual style is also by no means that of the horror film; all of the scenes, whether day or night, at forest locations or on cheap, unimaginative sets, are brightly, evenly lit, without a shadow in sight, without the slightest hint of mystery or of any expressionistic flair.

Where the presence of the horror genre does become most evident—and where the conflict between genres is most strongly articulated—is in the structure of the narrative. In very general terms, the film presents a classic vampire tale framed by both a western setting and by a number of relatively peripheral western plot elements. The progress of the film has to do with the ridding of the alien Dracula character from a western town and, on another level, with the ridding of a horror narrative from a western framework. A number of key western themes are established early on in the *Stagecoach* paraphrase cited above. Riding in the coach to "Wilksburg" are the comically somber Carradine, balding, alcoholic whiskey salesman Joe Flake (a kind of amalgam of Donald Meek's meek, bald whiskey runner and Thomas Mitchell's thirsty, boisterous Doc Boone), and a widow and her elderly bachelor brother James Underhill, a somewhat shifty-looking Boston banker whom we quickly associate with *Stagecoach's* crooked banker Gatewood. Underhill, we learn, has been induced to "give up his comfortable bachelor life" in order to come west and take charge of his sister's property along with, it is hinted, her daughter Betty; thus we have the theme of the eastern businessman helping in the development of the west by bringing out his business acumen, as well as some of his capital. A few scenes later, this "progress" is halted when, after an overnight stop, the stagecoach, like its counterpart in the Food film, is attacked by Indians.

These narrative affinities for the western, however, while self-conscious, also prove to be superficial. The Indians are not attacking out of a general sense of hostility toward the white man and his civilization; there in fact has not been a problem with Indians for ten years, according to one character. Rather, the attack and ensuing slaughter of all human passengers arises out of a minunderstanding of sorts: the vampire has murdered a young squaw and then disappeared, leaving the Indians to avenge themselves against the remaining coach riders. Significant is the fact that after the killings, the Indians are immediately dropped from the narrative, no classic western savage versus civilization conflict developed. The sequence functions instead more in terms of the Dracula narrative, establishing the vampire's introduction to and strong interest in a specific young virgin (Betty). Indeed, the later discovery of the coach with all its passengers dead echoes the discovery of a ship with its crew dead in a number of the films based on Bram Stoker's novel; in both cases the presence of the conveyance marks the vampire's arrival.

Also as in the Dracula narrative, the vampire's next move is to take possession of property near the new object of his affections in order to gain access to that object; in this specific instance, the vampire takes the audacious step of assuming Underhill's identity and thereby claiming title to the widow's ranch and guardianship over the newly orphaned Betty. Betty's fiancé Billy the Kid has similarly moved into Wilksburg's social realm, having shed his youthful criminal ways and taken a job at the ranch, and he and the vampire thus become rivals for social and sexual control over Betty, as well as rivals for economic control over the ranch that comes with her. The core of this narrative ultimately proves to have little in common with that of the western: Dracula does not appear to be posing a major threat to frontier civilization, even if he does let out a snarl or two. His interests in fact have little to do with either wilderness or civilization, operating as he does in an entirely different realm; he simply wants to bring his beloved into the world of the undead. Billy the Kid similarly functions as neither western hero nor western villain, his outlaw past ultimately appearing irrelevant to the structure of the narrative. He is not mediating between law and disorder or functioning in relation to some civilization/savagery polarity; he is just as much a part of western society as anyone else, with aspirations of gaining a stronger position (by way of Betty and her ranch) in the patriarchal hierarchy. In this sense, his generic affinities seem to lie more with the hero of the vampire tale—a young man trying to keep his lover from the clutches of the creature, the horrors of the netherworld.

Billy's main obstacle in achieving his goals is, appropriately enough, a new-world inability to conceptualize an old-world threat. Billy himself expresses a number of misgivings about the Osters' warnings, while Betty makes no bones about explaining to Eva Oster, "It's the nineteenth century, not the middle ages." Even down to the last minute, when Dracula clearly has Betty under some kind of supernatural control, Billy himself insists on firing bullets at the vampire; old habits die hard. The staking (scalloping?) of Dracula therefore brings about a two-fold resolution: Betty is freed from the vampire's spell and returned to Billy, and the western characters and setting are freed from the vampire narrative. The score shifts from horror movie tremolos to a lighter, more western-sounding theme as Billy carries Betty out of the mine, back into living frontier civilization.

The film's final image, interestingly enough, is not of the young couple, but of two old-time western actors—Olive Carey and Roy Barcroft—in traditional western roles, walking slowly toward the daylight; the image offers, for a moment, the same kind of nostalgic melancholy as do such late, transitional westerns as *Ride the High Country* (1962) (see Cawelti 513-14). What is ultimately the focus here is not the superficial romantic drama, but the issue of generic identity. The age of the western, *Billy the Kid versus Dracula* self-consciously reminds us, is ending, both within the dieresis and in terms of film history. The mine has been emptied, and its profits have been invested in a successful ranch; both outlaws and Indians have been co-opted by a prosperous frontier society. The drama has therefore been played out, leaving the shell of the genre susceptible to invasion by alien elements. We get a sense, then, that the presence of vampirism in the film functions as a manifestation of the decline of the B-western—the production of which had in fact never recovered from a 75% drop in 1959, coincidentally the year of the first appearance of a vampire western.[3]

Clearly, *Billy the Kid versus Dracula* is somewhat of an exception in terms of the emphatic nature of its compoundedness, yet even a more seemingly unified text like *The Harvey Girls* involves a level of interaction, of struggle between different generic frameworks. In order to achieve its greater degree of hybridization, *The Harvey Girls* must heavily utilize elements common to both western and musical dramas, yet it, too, has its rough edges where its compoundedness is more in evidence and it, too, derives a good deal of its meaning from the interaction between its two genres.

From its opening credit sequence, *The Harvey Girls* works overtime in attempting to simultaneously engage two sets of generic expectations. A western's images of a train heading west across expanses of land under an open sky are accompanied by a musical's overture of various song tunes, and one title, in typical western fashion, refers to the efforts which have been taken to ensure the accuracy of historical details. A printed explanatory text then attempts to situate the film's main musical performers—its title characters—firmly within a western mythological framework:

> When Fred Harvey pushed his chain of restaurants farther and farther west along the lengthening tracks of the Santa Fe, he brought with him one of the first civilizing forces this land had known. . . . *The Harvey Girls.* These winsome waitresses conquered the west as surely as the Davy Crocketts and the Kit Carsons—not with powder horn and rifle, but with a beefsteak and a cup of coffee.

Should this text not be convincing enough, the waitresses' supervisor shortly thereafter orally reaffirms that they "are the symbol and the promise of the order that is to come."

The business that these women help set up in the frontier town of Sandrock, a Harvey House restaurant, is indeed, on one level, a civilizing force, existing in moral and geographical opposition to the Alhambra, a saloon, gambling house, and brothel across the street from it. It would be quite problematic, however, to see the Harvey Girls as the female counterparts of western frontier settlers—or even as serving the same civilizing functions as the western's schoolmarms, for that matter. Rather than embodying any real "frontier spirit," they are trying to fulfill various personal romantic dreams, women from small towns across the country desiring to overcome the social, economic, and sexual frustrations in their lives. Their concerns thus seem much those of many musical protagonists. Susan Bradley (Judy Garland) aligns seeing a "new world" not with achieving freedom or gaining land, but with finding a husband, and her friend Alma's similar desires are clearly articulated when she sings "I was hoping to be roping something wild in the wild wild west," a lyric which comes near to burlesquing the western genre. For these Harvey Girls, the West clearly does not represent the unknown frontier so much as it does the realm of the masculine.

Susan Bradley's other key concern is in keeping the Harvey House afloat, in defending it from the attacks of those with a heavier interest in the Alhambra. While the film does set up the conflict between these two businesses as emblematic of an opposition between civilization and the wilderness, between two fundamentally different moral orders, it is also evident that the conflict takes place within the framework of an already established western community, within a town which could conceivably accommodate both kinds of businesses; indeed, the two men who most profit from the Alhambra have no qualms about the moral perspective the Harvey House promulgates, but are instead concerned about a potential loss of customers. These two men, owner Net Trent (John Hodiak) and his associate Sam Purvis (who helps run the town and takes a cut of the profits), are not, moreover, rough-hewn frontier toughs, but rather clean-shaven, well-educated, sly social beings, not that substantially different in their appearances from the manager of the

150

Harvey House. Susan does not know just how much truth she speaks when, in attempting to get on better terms with Alhambra prostitute Em (Angela Lansbury), she declares that their differences are "only a matter of style": both women are costumed and commodities to the benefit of Sandrock's businesses.

With Susan's struggles in romance and business as the central foci of the film, it is not surprising that the western framework so emphatically articulated at the film's opening proves largely peripheral as the film unwinds. Rarely do the western landscapes shown to us during the credit sequence again enter the visual field of the film or figure in any substantial way in the narrative's progress—save for in Ned Trent's secret desire to move to a remote valley, to escape what is indeed the established civilization of Sandrock. The story unfolds, rather, on the studio sets of Sandrock's interiors and streets, where the only fancy shooting which takes place is that of the camera. Little of the physicality or violent action—and none of the wilderness skills—central to the western are in evidence here. A hand-to-hand fight between the women of the two businesses is treated in a light-hearted, comic fashion, as is a sequence in which Susan utilizes two guns to retrieve stolen Harvey House meat. Most of the men of Sandrock, despite their sometimes straggly appearances, seem more disposed toward singing than fighting, and potentially violent or ugly conflicts tend to be resolved comically or musically. At the social dance offered by the Harvey Girls, these frontiersmen pick up the waltz with startling rapidity, and this dance scene, like the film's many other musical numbers, is covered in a seamless, flowing manner characteristic of the photography of numerous musicals, with extended tracking shots and often carefully disguised edits.

The character in whom the film's generic contradictions come closest to the surface is undoubtedly Ned Trent, who, as the film's leading male protagonist and the object of Susan's affections, is concurrently structured as a western hero and a musical hero. If John Hodiak's performance as Ned seems singularly inexpressive, it may be in no

151

small part due to the impossibility of Ned's character, simultaneously owner of the Alhambra and protector of the Harvey House, literate citizen and associate of thugs, engrossed with a particularly worldly-wise prostitute (Em) and wanting to marry a particularly homespun Ohio girl (Susan). Indeed, both of these women themselves repeatedly express confusion over the nature of Ned's identity and desires. These traits may remind one of Victor Mature's Doc Holliday in *My Darling Clementine* (1946), but we get no sense of any depth of character here, no picture of a tortured intellectual attempting to escape a painful past; rather, Ned is in a fundamentally ambivalent position, the western hero of a musical narrative.[4]

It is because of his alienness to the narrative in which he has been inserted that he can take few significant actions for the better portion of the film. He is, for the most part, merely a spectator, passively watching the comings and goings of the two women interested in him and of those interested in Sandrock's two major businesses. He cannot mediate, as a typical western hero might, between the realm of the Alhambra and that of the Harvey House because the two are so profoundly antithetical; rather than mediate, he must waver. He enjoys the social dance put on by the Harvey Girls, but dances there with Em and then attempts to lead his former patrons back to the Alhambra—only to shortly thereafter decide to take his business to another town and try to prevent Sam Purvis from burning down the Harvey House.

Sam does succeed in burning down the restaurant, although he is also beaten by Ned in the only serious first fight in the film, to the accompaniment of quick-tempoed music well suited for a western action scene. The next day the Harvey House quite literally takes over the Alhambra, moving into its former quarters, which suggests again the impossibility of any utopian compromise between the two realms, and Ned, although perhaps appearing a bit more heroic than before, is just as ambivalent about romance and business as ever. In the course of the final few minutes of the film, this Westerner wavers back and forth several more times before finally deciding to face the music, mounting a horse for the first time in the film and galloping after Susan.

The space in which Ned and Susan are finally rejoined is significantly ill-defined, distinctly outside of the limits of Sandrock, the realm of almost the entire narrative, yet also not fully into the desert, the ground here being covered with vegetation and clearly within easy reach of the town. It is a space existing right on the transient border of civilization and wilderness, musical and western, and it is the only space in which the couple can meet, a space Susan has previously described as "No place in this world."[5] she and Ned first fall on their faces, then traverse this lowest common denominator, this ephemeral strip of territory they can call theirs, before embracing. A quick fade from the embrace leads to a brief shot of their wedding ceremony, which is also evidently not within the main area of Sandrock, before the film ends. It is as though the utopian fusion attempted here must be absented from the screen as quickly as possible, least its insurmountable contradictions begin to surface.

In *The Harvey Girls* as in *Billy the Kid versus Dracula*, then, generic interaction proves a key factor in the shaping of the narrative. Certainly such interactions can serve widely divergent functions in different compound genre films, but what is important for the understanding of all of such texts is an examination of the processes of generic combination and of the implications of such processes in their given cinematic contexts.[6] Thus, while the two texts discussed here follow a classical Hollywood model in their tendency to resolve or disguise intergeneric tensions, the issues such tensions raise remain more pertinent than ever for such "postmodern" compound generic texts as *Gremlins* (1983), *Repo Man* (1984), *Raising Arizona* (1987), and *Robocop* (1987). Are disparate conventions neatly condensed in these films, or do they run amok? Does a given film put genre traditions into relief in order, for example, to expand on them, or to mock the Hollywood system, or to comment on a society which has itself coopted numerous diverse sets of filmic genre conventions as part of its own postmodern "reality"? Indeed, given the characteristic ideological slipperiness of many eighties compound generic texts, analyses of the kind suggested here can be particularly helpful in determining just how fragmentary a film truly is: Does a multiplicity of generic voices remain intact, or are discursive tensions nullified through a final large-scale condensations, a traditional unified resolution?[7] Such an approach can help us more fully get at the meanings that these films produce.

NOTES

[1]Susan Doll and Greg Faller, in their analysis of generic interactions in *Blade Runner*, have concordantly described "multi-generic films" as those which "do not homogenize their various conventions, thus failing to emphasize one particular genre and perhaps causing problematic generic classification for the spectator" (89).

[2]See Bakhtin 304-05, 358-66; see also Todorov's gloss on this material (73).

[3]The vampire western to which I refer is *Curse of the Undead*. Westerns produced by independents dropped steadily from 69 in 1950 to 16 in 1958, and then to only 4 in 1959 (Buscombe 426).

[4]I differ here with Altman's description of Ned as having a "surface personality" linked with the saloon which starts to give way to the deeper desires of a "submerged personality" (85-6). Rather, numerous contradictory, coexistent aspects of Ned's perpetually ambivalent character are evident throughout the film—a situation which I would argue is linked to the film's generic identity crisis.

[5]Feuer (72-3) and Altman (86,87) discuss the mediating functions of another related "no place," a valley which Ned dreams of moving to one day and where, on two occasions in the film, he and Susan can briefly meet in solitude and express their desires with relative openness. Feuer indicates, "The Valley synthesizes civilization and savagery, am-

ateur and professional entertainment, refinement and coarseness. . . . [It] is that place where the narrative dualities of the film may be worked out in symbolic form prior to the plot's resolution." While this is to an extent true of both the valley and the "no place" I am describing here, I would stress again that these dualities become confused in this film due to its fundamental generic ambivalence, a musical/western duality which simply cannot be fully worked out. It is significant, moreover, that the couple's final reunion takes place *not* in the valley, which is plainly emblematic of the wilderness and removed from the conflicts of civilization, but in a space which is less clearly defined and more transient, just steps from the railroad tracks which lead to and from Sandrock—a space not necessarily suggesting successful compromise between disparate spheres.

[6]For another example of such a reading, see Doll and Faller's discussion of how *Blade Runner* derives meanings by using science fiction conventions to "thwart the signification process of film noir" (98).

[7]Since the initial presentation of this paper early in 1988, there have appeared quite a few broad studies on the political dimensions of postmodern texts, a number of which have focused (in part) specifically on the ideological ramifications of generic fragmentation and/or combination in such texts. See, for example, Collins, Hutcheon.

WORKS CITED

Altman, Rick. *The American Film Musical.* Bloomington: Indian UP, 1987.

Bakhtin, M. M. "Discourse in the Novel." *The Dialogic Imagination.* Ed. Michael Holquist. Trans. Caryl Emerson & Michael Holquist. Austin: U of Texas P, 1981. 259-422.

Buscombe, Edward, ed. *The BFI Companion to the Western.* New York: Atheneum, 1988.

Cawelti, John G. "*Chinatown* and Generic Transformation in Recent American Films." *Film Theory and Criticism.* Ed. Gerald Mast & Marshall Cohen. 3rd ed. New York: Oxford UP, 1982. 503-20.

Collins, Jim. *Uncommon Cultures: Popular Culture and Post-Modernism.* New York: Routledge, 1989.

Doll, Susan, and Greg Faller. "*Blade Runner* and Genre: Film Noir and Science Fiction." *Literature/Film Quarterly* 14.2 (1986): 89-100.

Feuer, Jane. *The Hollywood Musical.* Bloomington: Indiana UP, 1982.

Frye, Northrop. *Anatomy of Criticism: Four Essays.* Princeton: Princeton UP, 1957.

Hutcheon, Linda. *The Politics of Postmodernism.* London: Routledge, 1989.

Jauss, Hans Robert. "Theory of Genres and Medieval Literature." *Toward an Aesthetic of Reception.* Trans. Timothy Bahti. Minneapolis: U of Minnesota P, 1982. 76-109.

Todorov, Tzvetan. *Mikhail Bakhtin: The Dialogical Principle.* Trans. Wlad Godzich. Minneapolis: U of Minnesota P, 1984.

12. EMBLEMATIC INDIRECTIONS: *BENCHES* BY TOM PHILLIPS

Erdmute Wenzel White

> "... our tuition is through emblems
> and indirections"
> Emerson

The *Ursonate* by Kurt Schwitters sustains the classical form of the sonata but exchanges notes for vowels and consonants of the German alphabet, keeping intact the elegant memory pattern of the sonata, a piece nearer the sonata-idea than the acoustic event itself. At once poetry and music, the dichotomy between conventional articulation and actual experience, between theory and fulfillment, defines new and unexpected complementarity. Meaning derives not only from actual display or mediation of the text but from a system of references and codes intentionally suspended.

Starting from Wittgenstein's "atomic facts"[1] and the idea expressed by Felix Volkbein in Barnes's *Nightwood* that images are merely stopping points between uncertainties of mind, I propose to study the sequence of (dis)incarnations of one single image, in this case the use of a simple park bench by contemporary British artist Tom Phillips, in order to illustrate how material manifestation may function at an enigmatic reminder of absent discourse. The effects of successive modification are most easily apprehended in the visual and static medium of photography and painting. Phillips, who is filmmaker, poet, painter, and musician, invites a reading which redefines formal elements and therefore draws attention to implied structural identity. Aesthetic procedure supersedes expressive criteria, reformulating not only genre expectations but allowing critical approaches beyond conventional comparative interpretation. The "discrepancy" between the arts becomes the semantic field for a new intertext.

In the tradition of Schwitters, such compositions as *Six Sonatas* (1967) by Phillips are visual sonatas or notations of musical painting. The 1968 opus 9 entitled *Ornamentik*, according to instruction, consists of a sustained note, "decorated" at ascertainable time intervals. Literature, music, and painting assume a purely theoretical presence as opposed to their physical figuration, reduced here to its merest trace. Phillips's work creates realms of speculative interchange and fugitive encounter, frequently produced by language itself. *Benches*, a painting done between August 1970 and April 1971, presently at the Tate Gallery, London, is a sequenced event, which comprises a wide range of media, including postcards, weaving, dance, opera, collage, film, Brahms (*A German Requiem*), and early Renaissance illustrations. The work, susceptible to being read as a three-page book with illustrations, enlarges the "performance" of the image, transporting one identical image through unexpected recurrence and transformation, turning a special figure, namely a park bench as emblem of mortality, into a life-giving sign, inclusive of and referential to all.

Tom Phillips writes of his passion for structure, connection, correspondence, and a system which seeks suspension of diverse elements within remarkable unity:

> my whole work is dominated by Coleridge's idea of keeping the greatest number of things suspended in a unity, the greatest diversity possible within a single thing: there, after all, lies the *imago mundi.*(*Works,* 62)

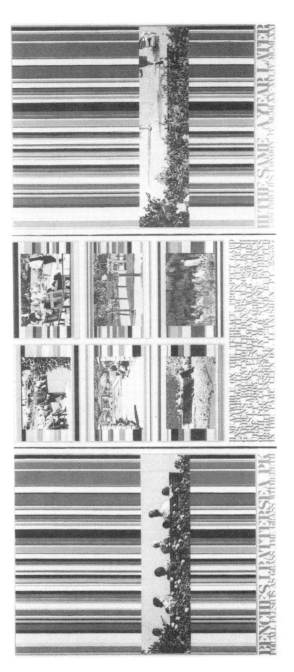

Benches by Tom Phillips (1970-71)

Battersea Park London PT8015.
Printed in Great Britain.
Publisher not given. Excerpt mag-
nified X10. (purchased 17.2.70).

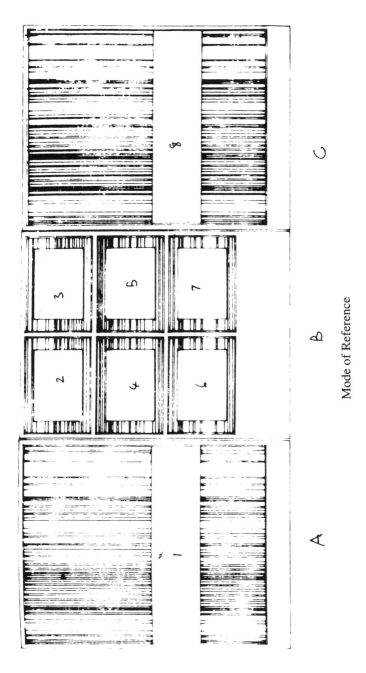

Mode of Reference

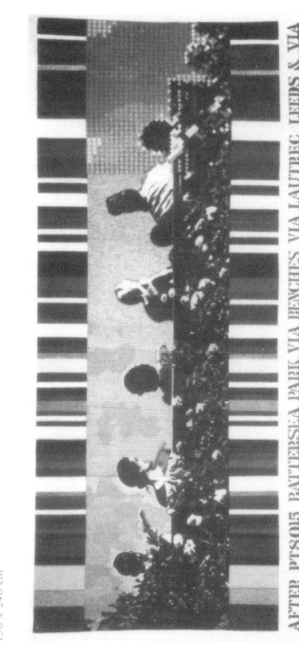

After Benches 1973
woven by Edinburgh Tapestry Co.
150 x 240 cm

His work entitled *Collage and Analysis* comprises two equal sections, a collage and its analytic reading. The collage includes photography, comic strip, a ticket for the Casino Municipal of Aix-en-Provence, swatches of paint, words left from a Victorian novel, and an engraving of a young woman, presumably a visionary saint, her eyes covered by atomic clouds. The lower part of the canvas constitutes a possible inter-text or theoretical blueprint of configuration and signs belonging to previous or future media events. The center of the collage, the young woman's face, remains suspended, barely perceptible in the analytic counterpart. Only ghosts, shadows, and geometry are left. The relationships between religious engraving and the atomic bomb suggests that our need for ecstasy is related to the dropping of the atomic bomb. The spectator witnesses an actual "entombment," a meaning extended here to include field of execution. While all remaining areas belong to different surface textures, the woman's face is an en-graving, a process which raises the topical element to topographic importance.

This cross-referencing between mental and physical worlds, their mutual reflection belongs to the order of "punning," an inter-mundium described by a pendulum of ambiguous terms and resemblances. While this art is visual, it is conceptual in nature. A perfect, almost random example of the detailed observation of process is found in the artist's use of the common postcard. According to Phillips, we expect photography to tell the truth, yet we also realize that the colors in postcards of earlier decades, the washed-out tints of the fifties, for example, which we took for realism, were color corrected and as illusory as today's products of imaging equipment. At each successive change and printing revolution, we believe to see more and better reality. Postcards record and freeze instances of what is to us real time. They belong to the order of documentary, are film arrested, single frames, and in Phillips's work, they are ultimately able to reconnect with movement.

Benches began with the discovery of a postcard called "Battersea Park" and seven further postcard reproductions of parks and public gardens. In each postcard a bench section was magnified and transferred to the canvas by means of paint. A short note on "dots" elucidates this method of transferrence:

> Where the images are painted in dots these neither relate to the true disposition of the dots in the postcard printing (although the postcards were studied with a magnifying glass of magnification X 6), nor do they follow any purist system of optical colour (unlike true pointillist paintings): they merely proceed from decision to work separated colour and the desire to be accurate [as process, that is]. (*Works*, 152)

The images were found by chance and selected for their "emblematic appropriateness." An emblem, a figure adopted and used as an identifying mark, includes the etymological resonance of an insertion, an inlaid or inserted ornament. In *Benches* the *ex*cerpts or details from the initial photos are themselves *in*serts within procedural color catalogues which surround them. The work which is built of three canvasses suggests a bird in flight, moving across categorical boundaries, a crossing which implies not only connectedness of diverse fields but a practice of presentiment and memory regained.

The initial postcard called "Battersea Park," used in images 1 and 8, by virtue of its name, implies peace and repose as well as agitation and doom. Life in Battersea Park is frozen to a gesture, sea and land are reduced to a wading pool and boxed trees. The cut-up, seated figures rise out of yellow and red roses. They are parked beings, evoking abandonment in space and time, their isolation and displacement enacted by their physical crossing from postcard to canvas.

People on postcards, according to the artist, are likely to be deceased by the time the postcard is purchased and belong to strategic moments of death foreseen. The images in *Benches* are referred to as "friezes," which dictionaries define as "sculpture or richly ornamental band and on embroidered cloth." The format chosen resulted from procedural guideline. Image 1, the artist determined, would conform to a system and its procedures would be externalized in form of a color catalogue. The abstract color catalogue, Phillips prefers the German "Farbenverzeichnis,"[2] is a notation of colors which are studio by-products, a kind of "scholarly apparatus." Colors are recorded in order of their use and further lists are made of grays which result from mixture of all colors left at the end of the week, called "terminal grays." The degree of procedural complication may be gathered from the fact that the separate colors used in *Benches* were submitted to systems of their own:

> when a green was used in *Benches* it was also added to the
> following:
> Das große Farbenverzeichnis
> Farbenverzeichnis; Chance and Choice
> All the Greens
> Synthetic English Landscape I
> Synthetic English Landscape II
> "Oh those Reds and Greens and Blues we used in the early
> seventies, my boy"
> Miniature Synthetic English landscape
> as well as being added to the general mixture for the five
> pictures being painted in the *Terminal Greys* series at that
> time. (*Works*, 152)

These procedural gestures are themselves emblematic, since they specify temporal identifying marks. They embrace all of life and, as in Phillips's "Projects for Infinity," may evolve into ritual dance freed from time.

The abstract and procedural sections in *Benches* are significantly larger than the figurative images, giving priority to method:

> This priority is only one of area since the colours, although
> they are ingredient to the image, are antagonistic to it in
> their solidity, clarity and verticality: they serve to empha-
> size the atmospheric frieze they both support and bear down
> upon. (*Works*, 144)

The abstract elements, that is the vertical color stripes, turn into a time-bound, momentary "atmospheric frieze" of figurative images. Both coincide in their common registration of time intervals as well as color sequence but not in form and suggest the weaving of textures or the swing from closed to open form. What is meant by priority of process becomes more apparent in a derivative work called "After Benches" (1973), woven by Edinburgh Tapestry Co. The large tapestry (150 x 240 cm) repeats the initial Battersea Park image, this time broken into small areas of varying textures. The tapestry thus records the visual event of taking form only inherently present in the formal difference between color catalogue and images of *Benches*. Exemplified by changes in methods of weaving, as the beat changes, the textural components and concordance of the image turn into see-through style, moving in and out of the eye, from figurative to abstract, stunningly visualizing the imaging of the image.

This distancing into "roughness," as we read from left to right, is rendered in its turn in a work entitled *AZ*, a woven color test or color catalogue of the Edinburgh tapestry workshop itself. *AZ* is the condensed version of the future tapestry frieze it announces. A frieze according to definition, is also a "heavy and durable wool and shoddy fabric with a rough surface." *AZ*, beginning and end, is the sea of life, in this instance, Battersea Park, as returned to its woven catalogue.[3]

Image 2 for *Benches* was chosen as an *Introit* (Latin: he enters), which is the entrance, such as a psalm, chanted at the beginning of mass. A man enters a magic circle of spectators, curiously resembling, as Phillips notes, the inventor of the cut-up, William Burroughs.

The artist speaks of the "elegiac tinting" of this card as opposed to the "Highly literal colour" of image 3, depicting people walking past benches, a card selected for its "processional motif." Image 4, showing a seated group gazing out toward an imaginary spectator, frames the spirits at the gate, with the viewer assuming Dante's and Virgil's position at the entrance of hell. The fragment of this image, as it is broken from the postcard, changes the suburban scene into a timeless Greek landscape with temple and reflecting pool.

Image 5 refers to the season of transparency. The original autumn scene is reduced on canvas to the emblematic sweeping up. Image 6, "In Old Steine Gardens," Brighton, is the most lyrical of postcards, depicting a couple floating against cascading fountains of water and shades. While they occupy the foreground in the postcard arrangement, they are the "absent ones" of *Benches*. The figures chosen for the canvas, waiting men on far away park benches, have moved into the "penultimate" phase toward oblivion. This idea is tangibly expressed by exemption of color. While the overall image is colorful, the seated, displaced figures are kept in black and white. Image 7 details a woman standing upright, evoking sacrifice and abandonment of hope. At the threshold of the underworld, waiting to pass below, blurred figures await total evanescence.

Half way through the making of image 3, the "procession," a second postcard version of "Battersea Park" was discovered. Taken a year later, at the approximate angle, it pictures the same bench, surrounded by red flowers but devoid of people. At this moment the formerly planned diptych turned into a triptych. The matching Battersea Park details now indicate not only two different temporal events, namely the present turned forward, but an interior theatre where both are variations of the same instant therein. Perceived through the narrow aperture of our time slots, the absence of the group of spectators corresponds to precise aesthetic procedure since image 8 is limited in execution to colors used in image 1. Paradoxically, while the final image is thus painted in "inappropriate" colors, so was the first image to begin with. Both, Battersea Park I and II are in turn united, neutralized in the color catalogue, which both "supports" and "Bears down upon" the visual moment, suggesting a dimension where absence and presence are equally true. Pigment of color and optical strategy announce a new, paradoxical cohesion, of suspension of mind, of interruption and withering freeze, visualized by the ballet-like hesitation of feet in Battersea Park II. We watch a mother and child leaving the center, acutely aware of terminal people and dying by fire. As flames of flowers engulf the vacant spot of waiting, tomb and place of child are one.

Benches shares its biblical citation, "For all flesh is as grass. . ., the grass withereth," 1 Peter i.24, with a series of engravings entitled "Ein Deutsches Requiem: After Brahms." *Benches*, a funeral hymn which stages resignation in the face of death, mirrors Johannes Brahms's 1866 choral work, *Ein Deutsches Requiem*, op. 45. There are seven movements in the Brahms requiem, set to a text from the Lutheran Bible. The beginning chorus addresses those lost in mourning: "Selig sind die da Leid tragen denn sie sollen getröstet werden" (Blessed are they that mourn for they shall have comfort), which is echoed in the last chorus "Selig sind die Toten, die in dem Herrn sterben von nun an" (Blessed are the dead which die in the Lord from henceforth). While the first chorus is deprived of brightness—clarinets, trumpets, and violins are banned—the first instrumental movement witnesses the breaking forth of violins, an intrinsic symmetry matched by painterly strategy which limits the last image of *Benches* to the same color sequence as Battersea Park I. In each case, there is a practice of blossoming forth and subsequent loss of surface, of subtraction and addition. The basic movement from absence to presence, from postcard to painting, to a ballet entitled "People on Postcards," where figures are allowed to melt back into movement, indicates a double force, at once holding and translating the movement of mind and eye, calling forth images seemingly unattached to matter. The artist investigates not a visual product but the structure of contingency or levels of contextual change as epistemological mapping system.

Benches refers to artistic events outside itself, externalizing an exchange between minimal trace and its fullest range of connectedness. The flower motif and central theme of *Benches* reappears in a text from Requiem movement, "Sie gehen daher wie ein Schemen" (Surely every man walketh in a vain shew), derived from Psalm 39. Phillips's illustration depicts people strolling among tulip beds, an arrangement which identifies flower and man. This central grouping breaks into surrounding images which in turn show business men in Düsseldorf and Frankfurt, men in insubstantial flight. Here the theme of absence is linked to men absent from themselves. As the chant for the dead continues its downward sweep, from the time-flower of *Benches* to supernatural motion, namely the motion of souls descending, the two left figures of the engraving actually cut through earthly space in order to reappear in Phillips's illustration of Canto 33 of Dante's *Inferno*.[4] The two infernal figures are again broken into halves, seen at oblique angles, separate but linked, their bodies clad in transparency. Like a vision made of glass, they belong to the batches of soul in hell's icy regions. When Dante exclaims at the sight of Friar Alberigo": "What you? . . . already dead?" the friar tells Dante that although his body remains on earth, "getting on there up above," his spirit resides in the underworld: "Oftentimes a soul can drop down here before it's been dispatched by Antropos."[5]

The dual twilight location of the Düsseldorf/Frankfurt figures, their presence in the requiem engraving, still among the living dead, and their simultaneous posthumous existence in the *Inferno* illustrations, associates visual knowledge with pilgrimages of the soul. In this dantesque sense of soulless phantom walkers (*Schemen*), their urgency carrying them into hell before their time, we may more fully grasp the Battersea Park movement between absence and presence. MEANWHILE, up above, on terraces and central gardens, people walk the earth in vain pursuit, or, as the inscription of the requiem illustration reads, "breaking grass and, scrubbing smoke" (*Works*, 170).

Absence, then, demands twofold vision, in the sense of "not existing" but also in the sense of "inattention to things *present.*" Although ostensibly made of color, the images in *Benches* reflect invisible color. They aspire to the substance of the color of ideas.

The texts for *Benches* were traced by means of stencilled letters found in the exuberant title piece for fifty recapitulatory paintings from 1962-1974. Each word unit of *Title Piece* is painted in different shades of terminal grays, reflecting a strategy already used in an earlier image made of six columns of acrylic color catalogues entitled: "Oh those reds . . . etc.":

OH THOSE REDS . THOSE GREENS
THOSE BLUES THOSE YELLOWS
WE USED TO USE IN THE LATE
SIXTIES AND EARLY SEVENTIES
MY BOY . YOU SHOULD HAVE SEEN
THEM . OH AND THOSE CHANCE
PROCEDURES AND THE ENDLESS
TOSSING OF COINS . THE GREYS
OH THOSE FINE AND INGENIOUS
CONCORDANT TERMINAL GREYS
MCMLXIX - LXXII . TOM PHILLIPS
(*Works*, 193)

Terminal grays, "fine . . . ingenious, concordant," mixed from reds and greens and blues, are at once containment and reminder of pure color. They are free from discord yet open to gradation, marking quiet atten-tiveness as opposed to active statement. Above all, they are in basic agreement (con-cor, Latin: with heart), contrary to the prismatic emana-tions or polarized contrasts of primary colors.[6] Terminal grays desig-nate colors of another order in that they are tones simultaneously heard. Consonant, they are equivalent to the muted chorus of the requiem, the absent presences of *Benches*.

If visual supposition and artistic gesture seem to render contradic-tory truth, namely that all we see is fabrication and color the archetype of illusion, there is also the perplexing instance of counter-evidence, a world not of void but of delay, where physicality spills into utopian re-solve. While the artist pushes to more extreme conclusions the materi-al's inner life, this exchange between artistic process and the eye's fixa-tion, functions as an internal commentary at the limit of sense. The im-age is submitted to a system which is oblique, evasive, indirect, slanted, not in direct descent, as visualized in the *Inferno* illustration. Truth is in formal cohesion.

Phillips writes about *Benches* that "the search was . . . not so much for images of the topos 'mortality' but rather for its emblem." This he meant literally, since the emblem, *emblema* (Greek: inserted ornament) and the cosmos meet, *kosmos* (Greek: ornament). The ornamental, superfluous, *Ornamentik* and the essential order of cosmos are one. According to linguistic lesson, life is the ornament of mortality is death's ornament. In this sense *Benches* scores the music of the spheres, is color of music, more precisely music with ornate figuration, to be performed like opus 9, *Ornamentik*, which comprises one single, sustained note, decorated at ascertainable time intervals, identified in *Benches* by the staggered stripes of color catalogues, filling in as "Gap map."

NOTES

[1] Tom Phillips, *Works . Texts . To 1974* (Stuttgart: Edition Hansjörg Mayer, 1975), 149. Henceforth cited in text as *Works.*

[2] The German *Farbenverzeichnis* not only suggests the making of lists and notations and the using up of color, but it includes the meaning of a drawing mistake, *verzeichnen.*

[3] ". . . if we weave a yard of tape in all humility and as well as we can, long hereafter we shall see it was no cotton tape at all but some galaxy which we braided, and that the threads were Time and Nature." Ralph Waldo Emerson, *The Conduct of Life*, Boston, 1860, p. 304.

[4] Tom Phillips, *Dante's Inferno* (London: Thames and Hudson, 1985), 267.

[5] Ibid., 270.

[6] Webster's dictionary registers under its entry for the color gray the old Slavic word *zireti*, to see.

INDEX

absence 166

Adventures of Augie March, The 52, 58

American dream 5, 49, 52, 57, 58, 59

American west 51, 53, 54, 95, 96

Bakhtin, Mikhail 1, 4, 9-10, 12-13, 18, 24, 28, 53, 142

Balzac, Honoré de 37, 38, 39-40, 43, 46

Barthes, Roland 1, 137

Baudelaire, Charles 89

Bergman, Ingmar 135

Bellow, Saul 52, 58

Benches 6, 157-168

Bible, the 5, 41, 62, 65, 71, 72n, 76, 84, 85-86, 165

Bicycle Thieves 5, 105-125

bilinguilism 21, 28, 31

Billy the Kid vs. Dracula 6, 143-149

Bryant, William Cullen 46

censorship 110, 111, 112, 113

center 86

Crime and Punishment 16, 18

collage 160

compound genre film 141-142, 153

Culler, Jonathan 19

Dante, 38, 163, 166

deconstruction 130

DeSica, Vittorio 5, 105-125

Dostoevsky, Fyodor 4, 9-19

Despair 4, 10, 15, 18

Double, The 4, 11-14, 16-19

Eisenstein, Sergei 5, 127, 129, 133

173

Eliot, T.S. 5, 76, 78, 89n

Exodus, book of, 5, 61-73

Fascists 62, 63, 110

Fernandez, Roberto G. 21-22, 26, 28

film scripts 5, 127-139

Fitzgerald, F. Scott 58

Flaubert, Gustave 11

Fontamara 5, 61-73

Formalism 137

Foucault, Michel 2

Franzwa, Gregory 53, 54

García Márquez, Gabriel 31, 35n

Great Gatsby, The 58

Gogol, Nikolai 11, 12, 13

Greed 5

Harvey Girls, The 142, 149-153

Heidegger, Martin 87

Hotel New Hampshire, The 52, 57-58

Hölderlin, Friedrich 5, 76, 82, 87

Hollywood film style 5, 105-125, 144, 153

horror film 145-146

Jakobson, Roman 137

Johnson, Barbara 75

Joyce, James 14

Kerouac, Jack 52, 53, 55, 56, 57

Kristeva, Julia 2, 9-10, 13, 53

Künstlerroman 37

Inferno, The 166, 168

intertexts, American 49-50, 51-52, 53-54, 59

intertextual imagery 119, 120

intertextuality 1, 2, 6, 9, 22, 50, 51, 52, 75, 86, 87; vertical, 13, 14, 15

irony 13

Irving, John 52, 57

Ivan the Terrible 139

La vida es un special $.75 21, 23

La montaña rusa 21, 23, 25

Lima, José Lezama 76, 82, 84, 87

logos 82, 87

London, Jack 52, 55, 58

Lost Illusions 4, 37-39, 43, 45, 46

Mallarmé, Stéphane 5, 76, 77, 79

Mann, Thomas 15

Martí, Jose 29-30

marxist fiction 61

McTeague 5, 93-104

Melville, Herman 37-38, 40, 42, 43, 45-46, 47n

Moby Dick 47n

modernism 16,

Moses 61, 65, 67, 68, 70

multimedia work 6

Nabokov, Vladimir 4, 9-19

Naturalism 94, 96

Neruda, Pablo 29

neorealism 107, 108, 110, 111, 113, 120, 122

Norris, Frank 93-104

nostalgia 22, 23

On the Road 52, 55-56, 57, 58

Oregon Trail Revisited, The 53, 54, 55

painting159, 165

parody 4, 10, 11, 13, 15, 16, 22, 95, 96, 98, 102

Phillips, Tom 157-168

photography 136, 159, 160

Pierre 4, 37, 40-45, 46

plagues 65, 71

poetry 76, 77-79, 85, 87

postmodernism 102

Potemkin 5, 6, 122, 127-139

Poulin, Jacques 4, 49

Quebecois literature 49, 51, 59

Raining Backwards 21, 23, 24, 25, 28, 29

realism 5, 96, 97, 99, 100, 109, 112, 117, 123, 127, 129, 135, 137-138, 160

"reality effect" 5, 128, 136

Riffaterre, Michael 51, 53-54

sacrifice 68, 69, 70

self-consciousness 3, 4, 5, 6, 142, 143

Selznick, David O. 113

sentimental novels 42

sexual symbolism 47n

Shakespeare, William 41

Silone, Ignazio 5, 61-62, 71-73

sonata 157, 159

Schwitters, Kurt 157

text, open 1

texts, biblical 3

Ulysses 14
Utopia 59

Valente, José Angel 75-91
Valley of the Moon, The 52, 55
Volkswagen Blues 4, 49-59
von Stroheim, Erich 95, 96, 99,
      100, 101

western 114, 142, 145, 147, 150
Wittgenstein, Ludwig 157

Zambrano, María 76, 78, 80, 81,
      82, 87